CW01638993

Public Relations and Corporate Communications Law in Ireland

Public Relations and Corporate Communications Law in Ireland

Damian McHugh

First Law

Published in 2006 by
First Law Limited
Merchant's Court,
Merchants Quay,
Dublin 8,
Ireland.

Typeset by Gough Typsetting Services, Dublin.

ISBN 1-904480-38-1

© First Law Limited

A catalogue record for this book
is available from the British Library.

All rights reserved. No part of this publication may be reproduced, stored in a retrieval system or transmitted in any form or by any means, electronic, mechanical, photocopying, recording or otherwise, without the prior, written permission of the publisher.

Printed by:
Johnswood Press Ltd.

Dedication

This book is dedicated to the memory of the late Gilbert Gough

Foreword

I have often heard it said that lawyers and public relations practitioners see the world totally differently. This is illustrated by the story of a corporate executive facing some crisis or other. He calls in his Head of Legal Affairs and his Corporate Communications Manager. The lawyer says, "Say nothing at all. Anything you may say could be interpreted as admission of liability." The public relations practitioner says, "Let me prepare a statement saying we apologise for what happened, telling them what we are doing to ensure it never happens again."

One advises black; the other advises white. Each believes that they are giving the best advice in accordance with the years of education and experience they have had in their respective fields. Up until fairly recently, the lawyer's advice usually won, because his salary was higher!

The dichotomy arises because both professionals are concerned with different courts. The lawyer is concerned with the courts of law. There is a world of precedent and rules to protect both sides in a dispute and it is the foolish claimant or defendant who does not use those precedents and rules in their own self-interest. The courts of law can be extraordinarily expensive places to assert one's position. Every advantage has to be maximised. This would certainly include silence

The public relations practitioner, on the other hand, is concerned with the court of public opinion. With growing activism among consumers, community groups and political entities and growing intrusiveness from the media, a wide range of stakeholders see silence as admission of guilt, and worse, as evasion, as arrogance and a lack of contrition. Evidence of these, however flimsy, leads directly to loss of reputation, the decline of relationships and the accompanying commercial penalties that come with them.

So which is worse? A massive bill from legal institutions in terms of fines and restitution or the loss of an organisation's good name, resulting financial losses and perhaps the decline of the organisation itself?

Of course, there has to be, and is, a middle ground. On this middle ground, the public relations practitioner's warnings are heeded. The good relationships which the organisation has achieved with customers, neighbours, regulatory bodies, professional associations, suppliers, distributors and political entities are all considered and action is taken to protect them, even if this means that candid accounts of challenging incidents are honestly and contritely published. On the other hand, those accounts should be crafted in such a way that ensures the organisation's wealth and resources are given the maximum protection.

Can such an ideal merger of perspectives actually happen and even more importantly, can it work to the advantage of companies? Well, according to some of the more recent public relations textbooks from the United States, there are indeed cases where companies have given due consideration to both the court of law and the court of public opinion and in the course of judgements, praise was directed towards the organisation for accepting their part in the issue at hand. Consequently, judges have made smaller awards against these organisations and the question of punitive damages was not considered. I have yet to read of a similar judgement made on this side of the Atlantic, but it certainly cannot be disregarded as a possibility.

Lately, there is evidence in this country of greater collaboration between professionals involved with law and public relations. There are Irish law firms which retain public relations counsel; others hire public relations graduates to provide in-house services for them. It is no new thing for public relations practitioners to seek legal advice on a variety of issues, but lately there are greater demands on public relations education, both in Ireland and abroad, to provide basic legal knowledge for graduates. Much of this is due to the changing tapestry of laws directly affecting communication issues such as defamation and privacy which are, as this is being written, under intense public debate. But there is also a perceived need that public relations graduates are people engaged in the business world and so should possess knowledge of contracts, employment law and other legal obligations which are common to all business people.

That said, there has never been a single publication which seeks to provide this knowledge in layman's terms. Those writing texts on public relations have always managed successfully to leave all but the most basic of legal issues for others to deal with. Unfortunately, those others have, for the most part, failed to come forth…at least until now.

Since well before my involvement with the Master of Arts in Public Relations Course at the Dublin Institute of Technology, future practitioners and journalists have been trained in writing skills by Damian McHugh. A former journalist with the much lamented *Irish Press,* throughout his time teaching writing, Damian has had to contend with contradictory pressures from industry for greater proficiency and professionalism in written expression and from students who no longer seem to receive disciplined instruction in writing in earlier education and therefore do not value it now. However, it was two years ago that I asked Damian to wear his other hat, that of barrister, to provide a Guest Lecture on Public Relations and the Law.

Damian threw himself into this with his extraordinary enthusiasm and lost no time telling me the "Mission Impossible" I had set for him to accomplish in a two-hour guest lecture. Later when our whole course team was working to re-certify our course's recognition with the UK based

Chartered Institute of Public Relations (CIPR), Damian was amazed to hear from Gerald Chan, CIPR's then Head of Education, that as with Ireland, in the UK there was no text dealing with Public Relations and the Law.

When Damian told me of this conversation, I replied, "Well, why don't you write it?" Having written a number of books which untangle legalese for the layman over the past five years or more, this was all Damian needed. I would never have believed that he would have the book written less than a year after I had asked that question.

The book you hold now fulfils a number of needs. For the student, it provides a text which is accessible, informative and enjoyable. It deals with communications issues and business issues, preparing the student for a bright career, equipping him or her with a guidebook to avoid the more obvious legal potholes which may be encountered on the journey. For the established practitioner who has not had occasion in years to update him or herself on the ever changing legal environment, this book will bring you up to speed, including a review of the recent debates on defamation, privacy and copyright.

But whoever chooses this book will be struck by Damian's ability to de-mystify the legalese which tends to turn off those of us who have not joined the law society or been called to bar.

This book reads like a conversation with someone who is not trying to blind you with science (or law, in this case) and yet so obviously knows what he is talking about. I think it is another book of which Damian can justifiably be proud.

John Gallagher, MA., FPRII
Course Director
Master of Arts in Public Relations Course
Dublin Institute of Technology

Preface

There seems little doubt but that the world of commerce has become more and more entangled in legal regulation. Becoming familiar with the many facets of the various laws that affect one's business in one way or another is a task in itself. The broad field of communication is no exception and, in fact, may be most affected in this regard. Once there is interaction with clients in a contractual sense and with the public in a general way, many different laws can kick in to affect the relationships between the parties. These laws are changing with the flux of time through common law development by the judiciary and by domestic and EU legislation. Good examples are the draft defamation and privacy laws which, as yet, are proposals. Defamation or libel reform has been in gestation since March, 1991 when the Law Reform Commission published its first consultation paper on the civil law of defamation in which it referred to the overlap between the law on privacy with that of defamation. That paper was followed four months later by the Commission's consultation paper on the topic of contempt of court. To date, there has been no reform by the legislature of these laws although we are closer to reform today than ever since the existing Defamation Act was introduced 45 years ago, due to the strong hand of the Minister for Justice, Equality and Law Reform, Michael McDowell, who not alone presented a Private Member's Defamation Bill while an Opposition TD back in 1995, but in Government has since guided the reform. Hopefully, the 1961 Act will not be celebrating its golden jubilee in five years.

The idea for this book came about in a curious way in the autumn of 2005. Because of this writer's involvement with the course of studies undertaken by postgraduate students of the MA in Public Relations degree at the Dublin Institute of Technology, Aungier Street, a meeting took place between the academic staff involved with the course together with the course director, John Gallagher and Gerald Chan, the then director of education at the UK's Chartered Institute of Public Relations. Afterwards, Mr. Chan approached me privately and suggested that I might write a Public Relations law book for students and practitioners as none existed either in Ireland or the UK.

Personal satisfaction by the suggestion and invitation to write such a work by a representative of such a respected body as the CIPR was quickly replaced by the thought of the endless hours of research, reading and writing involved. Rather than respond with a "why me?" question, especially since my most recent effort – *Buying and Selling a Home in Ireland* was still in the 'just published' shelves in the big bookshops, I talked over the idea with John Gallagher who reacted enthusiastically, saying that there was a need for such a work for students and practitioners alike. Who better then that John to write the Foreword for this book, given his background in public relations in the State and semi-State sectors, his deep involvement with the Public Relations Institute of Ireland and his dedicated work on behalf of students choosing Public Relations and public affairs for their chosen career paths. I am extremely grateful to him. I also talked the project over with my wife, Claire, the person who would be most affected, yet again, by my self-imposed incarceration in my study. Having obtained her imprimatur, the next step was to find a publisher willing to take on such a project. Bart Daly, managing director of First Law Ltd, was my obvious choice, even though the target audience of this book would not be the general public but a particular section of it. However, if First Law can publish so successfully for members of the legal profession, why not also for practitioners and students of Public Relations and corporate communications generally? Without hesitation Bart agreed and, consequently, the profession owes him a debt of gratitude for taking on this project, as do I.

With no precedents available, putting together the various strands of law that interact with Public Relations practice proved more time-consuming that originally thought. This book is as comprehensive and as up-to-date as possible. The law is continuously evolving and it would impractical – maybe even impossible - to include every possible piece of legislation that affects workers in the profession, even in an incidental fashion. There is a whole raft of labour law familiar to most people that does affect employers and employees but that very extensive body of law is not pitched at a level that this work is trying to reach. But there are developments taking place all the time. Such a development is a ruling of the European Court of Justice in Luxembourg last month that firms that pay workers in lieu of their holiday entitlements are breaking the law as these types of 'rolled-up holiday pay' schemes breach the EU working time directive. This directive guarantees workers rights to holidays and rest periods. The court's decision is a warning to PR and other firms with respect to their employees' rights.

The book is as up-to-date as possible in offering its readers a glance at the laws selected. However, it is not intended to be a substitute for obtaining legal advice when a problem arises. Therefore, no representation or warranty is given as to the accuracy or correctness of its contents. Most people are turned-off the law by the complexity of the language used by lawyers. As stated in the chapters that follow, the book is written in a consumer-friendly manner to make the various laws it addresses as understandable as possible to people with little or no knowledge of the many laws that could have a bearing on the practice of their profession. My hope is that it achieves that objective.

There are a number of other people who helped me along the way whom I especially wish to thank, not least Gerry Davis, chief executive of the Public Relations Institute of

Ireland and his counterpart in the Advertising Standards Authority of Ireland, Frank Goodman; Mairéad Collins of the PRII , Siobhán Early of the Gaelic Players' Association and Dudley Potter, solicitor, of the Chartered Institrute of Arbitrators (Irish branch), Clare Cochrane of the International Public Relations Association and Rose Fisher of the Bar Council's administration office for the small claims arbitration scheme. Also two colleagues formerly from the world of journalism but latterly very much to the fore in the field of public relations, Joe Murray of Murray Consultants Ltd and Bill O'Herlihy of Bill O' Herlihy Communications, not forgetting my former colleague and lifelong friend, Colman Cassidy for his valuable help at a crucial late stage. In addition, special thanks are due to fellow author and barrister, Dr. Neville Cox for his efforts on my behalf and most especially to Thérése Carrick for her once again applying her experienced editing skills to the manuscript. It is unfortunate but unavoidable to have to conclude on a sad note but that has become necessary because of the sudden death of Gilbert Gough just as he completed typesetting 12 of this book's 13 chapters. It is ironic that he should have produced the typesetting for the first book I wrote at the invitation of Bart Daly back in 1989, *Libel Law: a Journalist's Handbook*, which was meant to be a stop-gap pending what was believed to be the imminent reform of the defamation law referred to in the first paragraph of this Preface. As my tribute to Gilbert for his valuable work in producing this and many other books for First Law Ltd., this work is dedicated to his memory. Ar Dheis Dé go roimh a ainm.

Damian McHugh

Table of Contents

Table of Cases

Table of Legislation

Statutory Instruments

England

International Covenants, Conventions and Declarations

CHAPTER 1

Interaction with the Law

The first thing that needs to be stated is that there is no one law which governs or regulates the field of public relations and corporate communications generally. Rather is there a patchwork or mosaic of laws, some statutory and some common law, which practitioners or counsel will interact with in the course of their work.

A knowledge of law would hardly exercise the minds of most people working in communications in Ireland. But it should and it is equally important for PR specialists working in public affairs as lobbyists. Yet, in some countries, notably North America, a knowledge of law is paramount for practitioners while in educational establishments it figures near the top of compulsory subjects for students of this profession.

With the public relations industry showing steady growth in this country and throughout Europe, a general knowledge of the domestic laws applicable to the industry, at least, should be part of the skills of every practitioner. There are good reasons for this.

In the first instance, no person working in such a responsible profession which interacts with clients, with the media, with politicians, with administrators and the public at large should attempt to be his or her own lawyer. That is, of course, unless they have had some legal training. There is a very old saying which seems appropriate in this context:

> "He (or she) who advises himself (or herself) has a fool for a client."

It seems extraordinary in this year of 2006 that most second level students leave college without any knowledge whatsoever of this country's fundamental law, the 1937 Constitution, or *Bunreacht na hÉireann*, to give it its proper title, when it could, so easily, be part of a civics course for all students. Consequently, many of them go through third level colleges equally ignorant of the law that all other domestic laws are subservient to. Unfortunately, that absence of knowledge is followed through into working life for most citizens.

The areas of activity which the prudent adviser may need legal advice on are many and varied. It applies as much in public relations as it does in marketing, in advertising. It could also be very necessary in providing crisis communications advice. Therefore, even an elementary knowledge of a selection of this country's vast body of law should be part of the armoury of every adviser in this field.

Whether, on the one hand, in protecting oneself or, on the other hand, in being informed when advising a client, an elementary knowledge of some legal areas of interest will be no burden for the careful practitioner to carry through his or her career.

Unless a practitioner has had to accompany a client to court in a supporting role only, it is more likely than not the only time they will have been within the hallowed walls of the Four Courts or some such court of law in any of the country's major towns or cities. Likewise, if it has become necessary to interact with the media on behalf of a client who may be prosecuting or defending a civil or criminal court claim, even basic knowledge of our system of law – civil and criminal – will be essential to adequately represent the client's interest.

No Substitute for Professional Advice

For many people, the difference between the civil and criminal codes is blurred. Indeed, how many practitioners have sufficient knowledge of the courts themselves that they feel comfortable in advising a client faced with having to make a court appearance? That is not so say that there is no substitute for getting legal advice from a lawyer for a client with an obvious legal problem. But it helps the client's cause, and the practitioner's, if the latter is sufficiently knowledgeable to, perhaps, recognise that there is a problem in the first place and, secondly, knowing it is one that needs specialist legal attention from a lawyer.

A PR or corporate communications adviser may go through life without ever having to consult a lawyer, other than to engage one to effect a property transaction for home or office. However, given the litigious nature of society in this country in recent years, the chances of that still being the case in future years seems unlikely.

Special areas of legal interest

What legal areas of interest are most applicable to focus attention on for the purposes of this work? While such a list is not exhaustive, the following are certainly well worth inclusion:

- The legal system.
- The courts, particularly the civil superior courts, including the new commercial court.
- Contracts.
- Professional negligence.
- Defamation: Libel and slander.
- Malicious or injurious falsehood.
- Right of privacy.

- Employment law.
- The principal-agent relationship.
- Arbitration.
- Imaging rights such as the use of photographs of individuals and groups.
- Freedom of information and data protection.
- Intellectual property such as copyright, trademarks, patents and the tort or civil wrong of passing-off.

All of these legal areas are important to the independent PR adviser, consultant or agency in serving the needs of clients as well as, in some cases, their own needs.

Most practitioners in public relations, marketing and advertising, provide professional services to a broad spectrum of clients. If the practitioner is to fulfil his or her proper ethical role, the client will be advised on what they *need to hear* in any particular instance, not what they want to hear. Even a limited knowledge of some appropriate law will help them to fulfil that function to their mutual benefit. Indeed, even pointing them in the right direction or knowing how to source particular legal information can be just as rewarding.

Weighty tomes have been written about each of the legal areas of interest picked out here but it would defeat the purpose to present them to non-lawyers in the form of strict legal text.

No Legalese

There was a popular weekly American TV series back in the early 1980's called "*The Paperchase*" which focused on the college life of a number of students at a law school in California. On their first day in the lecture hall the students were addressed by a sour-faced professor of law who ruled his students and his department with a "rod of iron." He told them that they entered the college with "a skull-full of mush" but they would leave "thinking like a lawyer."

At a time when efforts are being made to give greater understanding of the legal process and the operation of the courts to the public as consumers it is important not to confuse them by the use of complex legal language.

How often have clients of the legal profession sat in court listening to solicitors, barristers and judges debating issues arising in their own case and failed to understand what was being said or, indeed, what was going on? There is only one answer to that rhetorical question, very frequently. Many people level their criticism at lawyers, not the law, accusing them of conversing in the presence of clients in a language that only they understand; that lawyers know this but choose to do nothing about, in the same way as doctors in hospitals are accused of speaking over the heads of their patients on ward-rounds. Mutual respect and understanding between professionals – whatever the discipline – and clients are vital qualities to good working relationships.

It is not the intention of this work to bamboozle readers into "thinking like lawyers", but to make them familiar with a selection of laws applicable to the industry they have chosen to work in. The language used throughout the chapters that follow will simplify as much as possible the particular laws under discussion so that practitioners will, hopefully, be in no doubt, as to their operation and effect.

A brief look at Some Areas

Arbitration is an alternative forum to a court of law to decide issues of dispute between parties. Alternative dispute resolution is a handy term to describe it. Unlike a court it is non-confrontational. Its use is on the increase for several reasons, not least because hearings before the arbitrator –

the person chosen to adjudicate between the parties – are heard behind closed doors, in private.

In the normal course of business – depending, of course, on the nature of the business or profession – a client may seek advice from a PR practitioner who has their account, before contacting a solicitor. This is far from being unusual. If the problem is one that lends itself to arbitration, then if the practitioner is informed about arbitration and the merits of taking that route, the client can be so advised. It is cost-effective and can be as well suited to the biggest as to the smallest claimant. In fact, one scheme launched recently is especially designed and administered by the Bar Council to deal with small claims, details of which are provided in a later chapter.

Defamation is an area that practitioners, like journalists, must be very familiar with because of the vast amount of copy that they issue to the media for publication. They need to protect themselves and they need to protect their client in doing so. And they need to protect the media. One of the things that may surprise practitioners is the fact that even though they may supply defamatory copy to the media for publication, it is not the client or the PR or corporate communications people who will be held to account if an action for damages finds its way to the Circuit or High Court arising out of its publication. Rather will it be the newspaper, the radio or television station or magazine which published the contents of the press release. But has the day arrived when the media will demand such suppliers of copy and photographs to provide them with an indemnity to protect them (media) in the event of a libel problem arising from it?

A working knowledge of the defamation laws is critically important for people who provide material for publication in the media. The dangers of libel lurk not only in ordinary news copy being transmitted to the media but also in advertising copy, in photographs, drawings and cartoons. Photographs can be a fertile ground for libel lawyers to mount actions. A miss-filed photograph, a mistaken identity, the juxtaposition of names, a file or stock picture of an individual or individuals being used to illustrate an occasion or event spells potential problems with legal consequences.

The tort (that is a civil wrong such as, for example, negligence) of defamation is an amalgam of different laws, one very important element of which – legislation – is undergoing change in Ireland. Reform of the legislation has been promised for many years but, irrespective of change, the basics of the defamation law cannot change and appears as such in a later chapter.

Professional negligence, as just explained, is a part of the body of law known as a tort or civil wrong. Simply, it means that a professional person has been negligent in giving advice or providing a service, as examples. There is a standard of care which every such person must adhere to and if that standard is breached with damages resulting for the person or person who received the advice, then the professional, such as a PR adviser, may be held liable. The question then arises whether people in PR and corporate communications should protect themselves against such a disastrous outcome by taking out professional indemnity insurance.

Employment law is a huge area which very much concerns practitioners both as individuals and as employers. There is a vast amount of legislation governing this whole area which makes the work of compliance tantamount to a nightmare for employers. Without regurgitating or reproducing the entire mass of law governing the area, the book selectively chooses some areas relevant to the PR and corporate communications advisers as employers themselves and also as advisors to their clients.

Within this sphere a number of institutions are extremely relevant. They include the Labour Court, the Labour Relations

Commission, the Employment Appeals Tribunal, the Equality Authority and the Equality Tribunal, which adjudicates on cases referred to it under the Equality Acts. In addition, the Equal Status Act must be considered because of the broad range of services it covers. The providers of those services are numbered among the clients of Public Relations practitioners and corporate communicators.

CHAPTER 2

Taking Care of the Client's Needs in Court

Having to appear in court can be one of the most traumatic experiences that a person endures in a lifetime. It is cold, clinical and foreign in the sense that it can be an almost out-of-body experience for some.

Parties to legal actions can quite suddenly decide to settle a case as soon as they get a whiff of the court on the day the case is listed for hearing. And that does not just apply to what might be termed simple cases. Far from it. Civil actions which were several years in preparation and which had legal issues as complex as they come are very often settled "on the steps of the court," as the saying goes. Cases that seemed impossible to negotiate towards a settlement, where the parties took up entrenched positions and were determined to have their day in court, have often suddenly been settled just prior to walking into court. In fact, there are few, if any, cases put together by lawyers which are incapable of settlement.

However, having stated that, no person should run away with the idea that every case that is taken at law will settle. Legal issues can arise in cases which require a legal contest in every sense of the word with argument by opposing counsel followed in due course by a determination by the presiding judge. However, it is a fact that the vast majority of all cases taken in the superior courts settle before, or during, the hearing. In rare cases, settlements have been reached between opposing sides after the hearing and before the judge gives the ruling.

Whether the client is going to court as a witness, as a

plaintiff or as a defendant (since it is more likely a civil action, a more suitable description of the party sued is a "respondent") the occasion can be a daunting one. Thirty years in Dublin's Four Courts as a journalist, and latterly, as a practising barrister, taught one to never over-estimate the effect an appearance in court can have on a person unused to the cut-and-thrust of the courtroom.

Being Familiar with the Language

Equally, one learned not to take-for-granted that people appearing before courts, in any capacity, are familiar with the language of the law and legal administration generally. For example, not everybody knows that a **plaintiff** is the name given to the party who takes a civil action and that a **defendant** or **respondent** is the name of the party defending such a claim. Why should they know? People lead busy lives and, realistically, it is only through some misfortune, bad luck or when it becomes necessary in the course of business or profession that they find themselves in court. Too often it is wrongly assumed, or taken for granted, that the general public know more about law and the legal system than they, in fact, do.

Different court Applications

Other things must be considered: the role of the Public Relations adviser or lobbyist when interacting with the media on behalf of a client who is before the court. The client may be a corporate client or a personal client, an individual, involved in some form of litigation. Litigation covers a very wide spectrum, including not only full-blown court actions but also a welter of other forms of court applications in the sphere of administrative justice.

This would include anything from an appearance before the Master of the High Court to get summary judgment in respect of an outstanding sum of money owed to a retailer, manufacturer or, indeed in respect of fees owed to a PR firm, a partner in that firm or a client of either of them, to an application for an intoxicating liquor licence for a club or restaurant or even for a new public house before a Circuit Court judge.

Motions

In between those possible scenarios, the company client may be faced with a restructuring under the Companies Acts and it may be helpful to the client's CEO to know that such applications to the High Court any day between Tuesday and Friday during the working week may be held in private or *in camera,* well away from the media and public gaze.

The court motion or application could be more serious for a corporate client. It may be an application on a Monday morning (when such applications are made) on behalf of a creditor of a company to have a provisional liquidator or a receiver appointed at the behest of a debenture holder. In either situation the PR adviser could be acting for the creditor or the company the subject of the application. Undoubtedly, with so much at stake for the company and its shareholders, the officers of the company would need all the positive PR they could get at this time of crisis.

There are other areas where the PR adviser may find himself or herself, or itself, in representing the client's interests which are not courts of law as such. These would include the Employment Appeals Tribunal where the client, as employer, may be defending a claim for constructive dismissal or unfair dismissal, or, alternatively, be bringing such a claim in the case of an individual.

Being helpful, not a Hindrance

The presence of the PR adviser could be most beneficial to interact with the media, if necessary. However, being available to the media should not mean that the PR or other adviser should become a nuisance to the working press, making a nuisance of themselves to journalists. As a result, efforts at achieving positive PR could have the opposite effect.

One recalls from the dim and distant past such circumstances when an individual sued a large multinational company in the High Court. The company's independent PR adviser attended the court most days during the protracted hearing. On each of those days he invariably visited the pressroom and usually asked whether he could be of help to the reporters. This "help" included providing glossy colour photographs and brochures of the plant at the centre of the action and press releases setting out the merits of the business. To put it mildly, the PR man's attentions were not welcome.

There is a big difference between being helpful to the working press and being a hindrance. The former will be beneficial to all concerned, the latter off-putting and defeat self-defeating.

Know when to Comment

What PR and corporate communications practitioners must understand is that court reporting – in any court from the District Court right up to the Supreme Court – is a very strict practice.

The word "reporting" is the operative word in this context. It is the factual reporting of what happens in court without any room for comment on the facts reported by the reporter. This reporting is governed by defamation legislation which provides legal privilege to the newspaper or broadcaster who publishes a report of the court case provided the report is fair to both sides, is accurate in terms of being factually correct, is published contemporaneously (in the next publication) and the hearing is in open court. Certain violations of that strict reporting could, conceivably, lead to the publisher being sued for libel or, indeed, the judge, or one of the parties to the action, initiating proceedings for contempt of court.

All of the foregoing does not mean that there is no room for comment by the media itself, or by the others in the media such as a PR or media advisor to a client, on the case the client was involved in some way. Of course there is but it cannot take place before the judge decides the case. This is especially so in the case of criminal prosecutions. The PR firm or practitioner is then free then to write and issue press releases on behalf of a client affected one way or the other by the court's findings.

It is stating the obvious that no attempt whatever should be made to try and influence the actual reporting of a client's case, and what subsequently appears in the media. It would be perceived as mischievous. To attempt to do so would almost certainly boomerang against the practitioner in terms of loss of credibility in future relations with the media and would do his client's cause in terms of public image no good at all. If the client wishes to issue a comment for publication on the *result* of the court case, then that should be done by the PR practitioner whose knowledge of the legal issues involved in the case will come in very useful at that stage.

Sub-Judice

Note the word *result* in that sentence. It would not only be inappropriate but could be construed by the judge adjudicating the client's case as an attempt to influence the outcome of the case and, therefore, be ruled as a contempt of court by the client and/or by the PR practitioner who issued the comment to the media in a press release. Until a case is finally ruled on with a judgment handed down by the court it remains in a state known as *sub-judice*. That means the case is still within the realm of the court. Extreme care must be observed. The effect of the case being *sub-judice* is that there should be no comment in the media about it.

Unlike in England, there is no legislation governing contempt in Ireland. Here it comes under the body of law known as the common law, or judge-made law, or the law of precedent, and it remains within the absolute discretion of the judge to decide how to deal with it in any particular case. Each cased is judged on its own facts and circumstances.

Reasonable Comment

We will refer to this again but at this stage it must be emphasised that such comment must be measured and be a reasonable comment on the decision handed down by the judge or judges (in the case of the Supreme Court). For example, it would be the height of contempt to attribute base motives to the judge or court by going behind the decision, as it were.

Press Release Contempt

If any PR practitioner wondered how the issuing of a press release could land its authors in hot water with the courts, they should pay close attention to what follows. Legally, the most serious form of contempt of court is that of "scandalising the court." That means undermining the very basis of the court's authority. Within memory there has been one such case which, by coincidence, arose out of the issuing of a **press release** to the media by two officers (both lawyers) of an organisation critical of a sentence imposed by one of the criminal courts.

Initially it involved one of this country's national newspapers which carried the contents of the press release on its front page but they were discharged from the case after the High Court judge accepted their profuse apology and declaration that in innocently issuing the press release they never had any intention of causing offence to the court or the administration of justice. The two lawyers were held in criminal contempt, a decision confirmed by the Supreme Court on appeal by the two.

That case is a precedent in this area of law and it serves as a warning to PR practitioners that they can never be too careful; that even a press release prepared by two lawyers can contain material that can fall foul of this particular law.

How to help Clients before Courts

Apart from the headline-grabbing big corporate cases, clients can also be involved in human interest-type cases before courts at every level. The same applies to tribunals, many of which have become almost permanent fixtures in this country in recent years. In the next chapter we will look at the entire hierarchy of courts but, for now, it is important for PR practitioners to realise that they can perform a vital role for their client by:

- Being informed – *in a very general way only* – of the practice and procedure of the courts,
- Knowing that they cannot, and should not, try to influence the reporting of a court case by the addition of material sympathetic to the client's cause and,
- Being conscious of the need to sometimes interpret proceedings or the outcome of proceedings on behalf of a client. This can be done by way of press release, for example, in language that the public understands. This will entail sitting in on the case and, afterwards, probably require

liasing with the client's legal advisers in order to be fully informed about the issues in the case.

No client would expect their PR adviser to be a qualified lawyer. All the better if they are. There are people working in Public Relations and corporate communications who have legal qualifications such as a diploma or degree in legal studies while others are fully qualified lawyers. This is all the more important if the client is a firm of solicitors, or law firms. A glance through the business pages from time to time shows that legal firms do engage people to provide PR and corporate communications services on their behalf both from the private sector while others head up their own in-house PR department.

This is a fairly recent phenomenon and one that can enhances the law firm's exposure nationally, and internationally if that is their desire. That said, an elementary knowledge by the average practitioner working in public relations and corporate communications of the rudiments of laws that may impinge on their own area of interest as well as a general idea about the workings of the courts, could be extremely beneficial.

Common Sense

However, whether the adviser has a legal qualification or not, there is one vital quality that advisers should possess. It is something that is arguably more important than all the qualifications a third level educational institution can grant. That is common sense. It is an essential component in understanding and practising law. This was brought home to me many years ago by an imminent member of judiciary who said that law was 75% common sense and 25% rules.

CHAPTER 3

The Legal System

A glance at the newspapers, local and regional, on any day between Tuesday to Saturday of the working week will show just how much reliance the media place on the reporting of courts at all levels, from the District Court right up to the Supreme Court.

The same is true of radio and television with one exception – their reports are broadcast on Mondays as well as on the other days. It is easy to understand why this is so: there is a prurient public interest in what happens in court, the good, the bad and the indifferent. It may be a neighbour, a friend, a family member who was before a court – civil or criminal – or just the fact that the headline on the court report was "catchy' and caught the reader's attention. It may have been something that appeared sensational, humourus or touched somebody's imagination for some other reason.

There is no denying the fact that whoever or other entity (e.g. a company) was before the court, the claim they are making or defending or business interest they are protecting, for example, has become public property as a result of being ventilated in open court and published to the public-at-large in the media. Because the consequences of this kind of exposure can be vitally important for clients, the more familiar the Public Relations adviser acting for such a client litigant is with the legal system, the better able he or she will be to offer advice.

Law and its Sources in Ireland

There is no one definition of "law." It has been defined as: "The just interference of the State in the interests and passions of humanity' and as a body or system of rules and principles that limit or prohibit behaviour in society in support of certain values or objectives. A law exists for just about everything, including planning, publishing, broadcasting, road traffic, divorce, copyright, to mention just a few.

The Constitution or *Bunreacht na hÉireann* is this country's fundamental law and one of the five main sources of law. The others are legislation, common law, European Union law and international human rights law. We will have a closer look at these sources in this chapter.

The Constitution

The **Constitution** was adopted by the people of Ireland in a referendum in 1937. The power therefore springs from the people – not the Government – and if the Constitution is to be amended, it can only be done by referendum. From 1939 to 2006 there were more than 20 amendments to the Constitution including, for example, the fifteenth amendment providing for the dissolution of marriage in certain specified circumstances.

The Constitution consists of 50 articles, commencing with a Preamble recalling the Christian nature and heroic past of the Irish people. Articles 1 to 39 deal with the organisation of the State. Articles 34 to 38 deal with the courts. The latter article states:

> "Justice shall be administered in courts established by law by judges appointed in the manner provided by this Constitution, and, save in such special and limited cases as may be

> prescribed by law, shall be administered in public."

The fundamental rights of the citizen are contained in Articles 40 to 44. These are also very important for the media and publishing generally, as we shall see in the chapter dealing with defamation. Other articles in the fundamental rights section deal with the family, education, private property and religion.

Common Law

Common law is basically a body of law built up through the centuries and is composed of decisions by judges in Ireland and in other common law countries, who laid down rules and principles appropriate to the cases before them. It is therefore also known as judge-made law.

Central to common law is what is known to lawyers as the **doctrine of precedent.** In deciding cases that come before them, judges look to the facts as proved in court, the oral and documentary evidence, if any, together with the law relevant to the matters in dispute. That may include decisions decided by judges in higher courts in Ireland in similar cases, *obligin*g them to follow the *ratio* or key principles that are relevant, e.g. Circuit Court must follow the High Court; High Court judge must follow the Supreme Court. However, they may follow, although they are not obliged to follow, the rules and principles laid down in courts of equal or similar level in the hierarchy of courts, Supreme Court. Also, judges *may* follow rules and principles established in lower courts, courts of equal importance or foreign courts. This is known as **persuasive precedent,** the one exception is the Court of Justice of the European Communities – otherwise known as the EU Court – whose decisions all Irish courts must follow, where appropriate.

LEGISLATION

Legislation is written laws or statutes which contain the rules regulating a particular matter. They are also called Acts and, as such, are Acts of the Oireachtas, the State's law-making body. One such piece of legislation is the Safety, Health and Welfare at Work Act which comprises the rules governing what is stated in its title.

There are thousands of Acts on the statute book which can be viewed on the Government's website: www.irlgov.ie, most of which were made by the Oireachtas. Just over 40 Acts were signed into law by the President (*Uachtarán na* hÉireann) in 2004.

There are also some old Free-State laws still in existence. These relate from 1922; one such is the Censorship of Publications Act 1929, which established the Censorship of Publications Board. It also prohibits the reporting of certain types of court applications.

There is also pre-1922 legislation on the statute book in this country. One of the most used of these is the 1861 Offences Against the Person Act which operated in this country and in England. In fact, in 2005, an English citizen was put on trial in London and found guilty of the murder of an Irish woman. What was unique about the trial was the fact that the murder was committed in Dublin. The Crown Prosecution Service used a little-known section of the 1861 Act to put him on trial in England for a murder committed abroad.

In addition to Acts, there is a body of secondary or delegated legislation called Statutory Instruments which provide the details or nuts and bolts not carried in the Acts to which they relate. The main Act must authorise the subordinate legislation for the secondary legislation and what's contained in it to be valid.

EU Law

EU Law is an important source of law and has greater impact on the life of citizens than is generally realised. It came about as a result of this country's accession to the EEC in 1973. The 1937 Constitution was amended to provide for it. Membership obliges each of the 25 States to be bound by the various treaties which implement the laws.

The laws take different forms. They are **Regulations, Directives, Decisions, Recommendations** and **Opinions**. The two most important are regulations and directives. **Regulations** are directly binding in Ireland the other member states while **Directives** are laws that all member states must bring into effect by introducing domestic legislation containing the particular EU law and do so within a prescribed time frame. Failure to implement the law within the time allowed may result in the member state being taken by the EU Commission before the EU Court in Luxembourg.

Occasionally the Commission will permit Member States an extension of the time limit in order to prepare for the implementation of the new law. An example is the Energy Performance of Buildings Directive which was due to be transposed into domestic law on January 4, 2006, but a further three years for implementation was permitted "because of a lack of qualified and/or accredited experts." Apart from the Commission and the court, the other main EU institutions are the Council of Ministers, which is the main decision-making body, the European Parliament, which usually sits for one week in every month in Strasbourg, France, and the Court of Auditors which supervises budget spending.

Human Rights Law

Human Rights Law is a developing body of law in this country, much of it arising out of High Court judicial review applications and appeals by asylum seekers. However, this law is likely to be more widely availed of to establish an alleged violation of rights by the State or State agencies, for example, in the future.

The origin of this law lies in the fact that Ireland has ratified a number of international treaties, covenants or conventions which seek to ensure minimum standards in the protection of human rights. These include the UN Declaration of Human Rights, the International Covenant on Civil and Political Rights and, notably, the European Convention on Human Rights which was adopted in 1950 by the Council of Europe, the first European political organisation which was born from the debris and the barbaric acts of the second world war.

This council should not be confused with the EU Council of Ministers, an altogether different organisation. Under the Convention, which came into force in 1953, Ireland the other States, which number more that 50, guarantee basic civil and political rights of a State governed by the rule of law, not only to their own citizens, but to all persons "within their jurisdiction."

Heretofore, States or individuals could bring a complaint before the European Court of Human Rights in Strasbourg set up by the Convention. They still can but since 2003 the Convention has been given the force of law by the enactment of the European Convention on Human Rights Act which incorporates into the legislation the Convention for the Protection of Human Rights and Fundamental Freedoms, to give it its proper title. As a result, any person who suffers injury, loss or damage as a result of a contravention of the State's obligations under the Convention's provisions, may bring proceedings in the High Court or the Circuit Court, depending on the monetary amount of the claim, rather than going to Strasbourg. In April, 2004 in a decision in the High Court, Miss Justice Mary Laffoy ruled that the ECHR Act 2003 did not directly incorporate the European Convention on Human Rights into Irish law. However, it did create statutory rights that were parallel to those in the Convention.

Some of the Convention's articles are similar to the guarantees or protections of certain rights in the 1937 Constitution – albeit some are implied – including, right to a fair trial, right to life, freedom of expression (Press freedom), right to respect for private and family life, right to marry, freedom of assembly and association. Others are not but are to be found in legislation in different forms in this country, including prohibition on discrimination. This is article number 14 in the Convention which states:

> "The enjoyment of the rights and freedoms set forth in this Convention shall be secured without discrimination on any ground such as sex, race, colour, language, religion, political or other opinion, national or social origin, associated with a national minority, property, birth or other status."

Some Personnel of the Law

Practitioners and students should know about the different legal professionals operating in the Irish legal system in order to essentially advise clients. There are two branches of the legal profession, solicitors and barristers. They perform distinctly different functions. When a person has what seems to be a legal problem and requires advice, they will first need to consult a solicitor. As yet, barristers are generally not permitted to take instructions directly from a member of the public although this is likely to change, to some limited extent, in the near future. They only give legal advice after receiving instructions from a solicitor acting for a client. So, strictly speaking, the client is a client of the solicitor, not of the barrister.

- **Solicitors** may practice as a sole practitioner, belong to a firm or form a partnership as a firm of solicitors, many of which exist throughout the country. A member of the public is free to walk into any solicitor's office, make an appointment and meet a solicitor to discuss a problem, have a will executed or the estate of a deceased person administered, a property purchased or sold by a solicitor specialising in conveyancing or a multitude of other tasks that the solicitor is expert in carrying out under the client's instructions. The prospective client is entitled to ask for the cost of, or an estimate of, the work to be carried out and the solicitor is legally obliged to provide that information. The Law Society, situated at Blackhall Place, Dublin 7, is the educational, representative and regulatory body of the solicitors' profession, exercising its functions under legislation in relation to the education, admission, enrolment, discipline and regulation of the profession. There are some 6,700 solicitors in practice in this country at present.

- **Barristers** If the instruction involves a matter requiring a court application, and the solicitor feels competent to carry out that function, he or she is perfectly entitled and trained to do so. If the issue or problem is more complex and requires further specialised legal research, then a barrister or counsel, as they may be also referred to as, may be instructed by the solicitor to give a written advice in the first instance, to prepare the case for court – if the client so wishes after being informed of counsel's opinion – and then to act as advocate at the court hearing. The barristers' branch of the legal profession is collectively known as the Bar. The Honourable Society of King's Inns, located at Henrietta Street, Dublin 1, provides post-graduate legal training for those who wish to practice at the Bar. There are about 1,540 practising barristers in the country, many of whom operate from the Law Library in the Four Courts,

Dublin; others from Cork, Galway and other centres who practice on the various circuits into which the country is divided. They are prohibited by a strict code of conduct from touting for business. This, among other reasons, ensures the much-valued independence of the Bar. In court during the law terms, barristers are attired in dark clothing, including a gown, white shirt with winged collar, white blouse in the case of female barristers, and a white band. The wearing of a wig, which used to be mandatory, is now at the discretion of the barrister. A distinction exists in the Bar between junior counsel and senior counsel. A barrister is conferred with the degree of Barrister-at-Law which appears after his or her name as such or as BL for short. The rules of the Bar require that in order to become a senior counsel – or member of the Inner Bar – only persons of "professional eminence" should be admitted. The general conduct of barristers is conducted by the General Council of the Bar of Ireland, a non-statutory body.

Attorney General The AG is the legal adviser to the Government in matters of law and legal opinion and scrutinises all draft legislation before it is presented to the Houses of the Oireachtas. He cannot be a member of the Government and is appointed by the President on the nomination of the Taoiseach. By convention the Attorney, who has always been a member of the Inner Bar, ranks as the most senior member of the Bar and is known as the leader of the Bar. The role of Attorney General is provided for in Article 30 of the Constitution.

Legal Services Ombudsman This is the name of a *proposed* new entrant to personnel of the law whose role will be to oversee the handling by the Law Society and the Bar Council of complaints against solicitors and barristers of inadequate services, excessive fees and misconduct. The key functions of the proposed Ombudsman are:

(a) providing a forum of appeal for clients of solicitors or barristers who are dissatisfied with the outcome of complaints made to the Law Society or Bar Council,

(b) an overseeing role by examining a selection of complaints' files each year taken on a random basis, and

(c) monitoring access to the professions and reporting to the Minister for Justice and the Oireachtas on the adequacy of numbers admitted annually to each profession.

CHAPTER 4

The Courts' System

It is important to know that there are two distinct aspects to the law in this country. There is civil law and criminal law. Very often the distinction between the two is sufficiently blurred that a person can walk into a court dealing with a civil matter but fail to realise it is, in fact, the hearing of a criminal matter. This chapter is devoted to the various courts and explains the jurisdiction or power they have to deal with specific matters or issues.

This power in the civil courts is allocated on two very different bases. There are strict limits on the amount of money the lower courts – the District Court and Circuit Court – can award by way of compensation or as damages and there are limits on the type of issues or subject matter which the different courts in the hierarchy of courts can deal with, e.g. the District Court has no power to deal with libel actions, but the Circuit and High Courts have. On the criminal side, the lower the court, the less serious the offences they have power to handle.

The courts which make up the hierarchy of courts are: the District Court, Circuit Court, High Court, Special Criminal Court, Court of Criminal Appeal and the Supreme Court. Only two of them are mentioned by name in the Constitution, the High Court and Supreme Court. The rest are "creatures of statute," that is they were brought into existence by Acts of the Oireachtas. Our examination of the courts will start with the court on the lowest rung of the ladder, the District Court, a division of which is the Small Claims Court.

The Small Claims Court

This court is of great importance to consumers who can bring a claim before the court, lose it and not have to worry about having to pay any legal costs. It is the most consumer-friendly court in the country and costs just €9 to get a case before the judge, who is an ordinary judge of the District Court.

In some areas of the country, claims are brought before a judge who takes the case as part of a full-day's list. In Dublin, the court sits exclusively as a Small Claim Court for one or two days every week of term in Court No.54 in the Richmond Buildings, off Church Street, about a 10-minute walk from rear of the Four Courts. The maximum amount of the claim cannot be greater than €1,269.74 (£1,000 in old currency) although the Consumer Strategy Group, established by the Minister for Enterprise, Trade and Employment to make proposals for the development of a national consumer strategy, in their report published in 2005 adopted the recommendation of this author in his book, *The Small Claims Court in Ireland – A Consumer's Guide* (First Law, Dublin, 2003) to have this figure increased to a more realistic limit of €3,000.

In order to bring a claim, a person as consumer must have bought the goods or services from somebody selling or providing them in the course of business. Excluded from the procedure are claims in respect of matters related to rented accommodation such as the return of a deposit or key money, hire-purchase agreements, leasing agreements and debts. Also excluded are claims for personal injuries.

A person bringing a claim can download a form from the courts' website at www.courts.ie, complete it and submit it to the staff in the appropriate District Court office. The staff there will help the person to complete the form. Subsequently, one of Registrars of the court will try and effect a settlement between the parties and it is only if that fails to materialise that the case will go before the judge for a hearing. Although it is meant to be a lawyer-free procedure, it is possible that a person can turn up in court all ready to present their case only to find that the respondent is represented by a solicitor, and sometimes by both a solicitor and barrister.

After hearing the evidence of both sides in a normal claim the judge will make a decision. No costs will be awarded to either side. The losing party can appeal to the Circuit Court where solicitor and counsel will usually be involved and the normal rules will apply – costs will be awarded against the unsuccessful party.

The District Court

The country is divided up into 23 districts –one of them the Dublin Metropolitan District – for the purposes of the operation of the District Court, which has 55 judges. In dealing with *civil* cases the court is limited on two grounds: the amount of money it can award in any one case, and the type of matter it can deal with. In cases of contract and tort (*i.e.* a civil wrong, such as negligence in causing a road accident), the court may only award a maximum of €6,3498.69 (IR£5,000 in old currency). Rounded off this is €6,350.

It also deals with intoxicating liquor applications where objections have been filed to a licence renewal, family law applications such as maintenance of spouses and children (within monetary limits of €500 a week to a spouse and €150 a week for a child) and power to enforce payment, also environmental protection applications such as noise abatement and a multitude of other matters that it is empowered by legislation to deal with.

On the *criminal* side, the court deals with an enormous amount of offences, the vast bulk of which are known as summary or minor offences such as simple assault or careless driving of a motor vehicle, in which the accused is not entitled to trial by a judge and jury. The second category would be indictable offences which the court can deal with provided the accused and the Director of Public Prosecutions (DPP) consent to it and the judge is satisfied that the facts of the crime constitute a minor offence.

The third category is concerned with the trial of certain indictable offences (excluding murder, rape, aggravated assault, treason and piracy) where the accused pleads guilty, the DPP consents and the judge accepts the guilty plea. If either party refuses, the judge will send the accused forward on his plea of guilty for sentencing to the Circuit Court judge.

The fourth category is concerned with those serious offences in which a Book of Evidence (composed of witness statements and other documentary evidence) prepared by the prosecution is served on the accused within 42 days of first appearing before the court. The judge will consider the evidence together with submissions by the defence and prosecution. If the judge decides that there is a *prima facie* case, *i.e.* that the accused has a case to answer, the accused will be sent forward for trial to the Circuit Court or the Central Criminal Court to be tried in a full-blown trial by judge and jury. The court also has power to make safety and barring orders in the case of domestic violence. An accused convicted by the District Court may appeal against the conviction and/or the sentence or penalty, if any, to the Circuit Court where a judge will retry the accused who faces the prospect of an increased sentence or penalty if the appeal fails.

Conduct of a Hearing

The conduct of the hearing of a *civil* action in the District Court is straightforward. The plaintiff is represented by a solicitor who "opens" the case by giving a brief outline of the basis of the claim. The plaintiff is usually the first witness called to give direct evidence – answering questions posed by his or her own solicitor – and is then cross-examined on that evidence by the solicitor for the other side, the defendant or respondent.

The plaintiff's own solicitor may then ask some questions arising out of the cross-examination. If the plaintiff has more witnesses, they are then called and questioned and cross-examined in the same way. The judge may also ask questions in order to clarify some evidence or issue.

The burden of having to prove his or her case lies on the plaintiff. That standard that the law requires is to establish the claim on the balance of probabilities. If the judge feels that the plaintiff has not discharged that standard, the case will be dismissed at that point. If not, then the defence opens. The defendant or respondent is called to give evidence, is cross-examined by the plaintiff's solicitor.

The hearing proceeds in the same way and at the conclusion of the evidence, the solicitors for both parties may address the judge on the evidence and possibly make legal submissions in support of the case or in defence of the claim. The judge then delivers a decision and awards costs to the successful party against the unsuccessful one.

A party who loses a claim may appeal to the next court up, the Circuit Court which re-hears the case. The other avenue of appeal is for one of the parties to the action to ask the judge to state a case for the opinion of the High Court. This is called a Case Stated. The judge writes a report of the case, including a brief summary of the evidence, the law, if any, presented to the court, and the ruling. This is heard by a High Court judge on some Monday when the parties are represented usually by solicitors and counsel. The parties to the case are not called to give evidence; rather is it put into a sworn statement called an affidavit which is read to the judge. Legal submissions are made and the judge reserves judgment, meaning that he or she will prepare a written report of the decision and the reasons for it. This will be handed down on a later date.

The losing party has a right of appeal to the Supreme Court. Therefore, a small claim which started out in the lowest court can end up in the highest court in the country, the Supreme Court. Because of the doctrine of precedent that was referred to in an earlier chapter, the ruling of the higher court binds the District Court judge who must apply the law as either the High Court or Supreme Court laid down.

Another procedure that a losing party can take to test the District Court judge's ruling in both a civil claim and in a criminal prosecution is to bring an application for **judicial review** directly to the High Court. This is not an appeal but a procedure under which the higher court will review the decision of the lower court. The procedure is much the same as a **case stated,** where the parties and their witnesses put their evidence on affidavit for the High Court judge to review and to consider the law as submitted orally and in writing by counsel for both sides. A decision in the form of a written judgment is given at a future date. Again, there can be an appeal to the Supreme Court.

Circuit Court

Like the District Court, the Circuit Court is presided over by one judge known as the President. There are 33 judges presiding in eight circuits into which the country is divided, with one judge assigned to each circuit but large urban areas like Dublin and Cork have many Circuit Courts – civil and criminal – and therefore require many judges to administer the law. Again, like the District Court, it is not mentioned by name in the Constitution and only has power to deal with the matters assigned to it by legislation. Robed – and sometimes wigged – barristers or junior counsel, who are instructed by solicitors, normally appear for litigants. Senior counsel do not normally appear in civil actions in the Circuit Court but clients are free to instruct their solicitor to engage senior and junior counsel if they feel or are advised of the need to.

Civil

In civil cases there is a monetary limit of €38,092 on the amount of money it can award. However, the parties to an action can confer unlimited power on the court in awarding money if they agree to it and put this consent in writing in a prescribed form before the case starts. In land disputes – of which there are many – the court has power to deal with it where the poor law valuation of the property does not exceed €254. This also applies in other types of cases such as where the court is ruling on a case where a partnership is being dissolved, a case arising out of the partition or sale of land. The plv qualification also applies to two other types of cases which come before the Circuit Court, injunctions and specific performance.

Injunctions arise where, for example, one party asks the court to make an order to stop another party from trespassing on the first party's property. However, the injunction is ancillary to the main action which in this case would be for damages for trespass. Specific performance arises where a party asks the court for an order so named to compel another party to complete the obligations agreed in a contract for the purchase or sale of property.

The court deals with a considerable amount of landlord and tenant issues, intoxicating liquor applications and family law. It has the same or concurrent power or jurisdiction with the High Court to hear cases of judicial separation and divorce.

In fact, on any one day, three judges will sit, in Courts Nos 30, 31 and 32, in Phoenix House, Phoenix Street North, Smithfield, Dublin 7 to deal with about 50 cases, many of which would be related to divorce applications. At the same time, three other judges are sitting in courts in the main Four Courts complex dealing with about 23 matters, including trials, motions and matters for mention only. PR advisers should note that when a case is supposed to take a day, an hour or a week to hear, judges say that realistically they will take double the time allotted. In other words, if the lawyer tells the judge it is estimated that the case will take a half-day to hear, it will, in fact, take the entire day.

In all Circuit Court civil actions the judge sits *without* a jury. This applies even in actions for damages for defamation, even though in a similar action in the High Court – albeit a claim for unlimited damages – a jury is empanelled to try the case with a judge. Appeals are heard by a High Court judge but there is a procedure – similar to the **case stated** procedure in the District Court accept it is called a **consultative case stated** – in which the Circuit Court judge may ask the Supreme Court – not the High Court – for its opinion on a point of law that arose. The response usually determines the action at hearing in the Circuit Court.

Criminal

A jury only sits in the Circuit Court in *criminal* trials where the State carries the burden of establishing the accused's guilt beyond a reasonable doubt. PR and communications practitioners and students should realise that the golden thread which runs through the criminal law in this country is that a person charged with having committed a criminal offence, of any nature, is deemed innocent by the law until he or she is proved guilty by the State. The accused is entitled to the presumption of innocence.

When a person is brought before the Circuit Court for trial, the court registrar reads out the charge and the accused is asked how he or she is pleading, guilty or not guilty. This is called an arraignment. If the accused pleads "guilty', there will be no trial as such. The jury will not be involved. The prosecution give an outline of the offence and details of the accused's background and criminal record, if any, and the judge passes sentence.

However, if a plea of "not guilty" is entered, a trial will follow, not necessarily that day but on some day in the near future when a jury will be sworn in especially to try it. The trial follows the same procedure as in the District Court (above) accept in this case the jury decides on the guilt of the accused, not the judge. However, as with the District Court, it is for the judge to decide the penalty if there is a "guilty" verdict.

If convicted, the defendant has a right of appeal against the conviction and/or any penalty or prison sentence that may have been imposed. So also may the Director of Public Prosecutions appeal but on one ground only, that the sentence imposed by the judge was unduly lenient.

These appeals, in addition to any alleged miscarriage of justice case, go to the **Court of Criminal Appeal**, a court composed of a Supreme Court judge and two High Court judges, which sits on Mondays to hear appeals composed entirely of examining the transcript of the trial, the judge's charge to the jury and hearing legal submissions. The court does not take oral evidence from witnesses. It may sit on a later date and on some other day of the week to hand down a written judgment in a particular appeal. Very occasionally and in very special circumstances there can be an appeal to the Supreme Court on a point of law of exceptional public importance arising out of the appeal hearing in the CCA.

The High Court

All claims for damages in excess of €38,092 will go to the High Court, a court with unlimited power or jurisdiction in all types of claim or issue of fact or law, civil or criminal. It is administered by the President and 31 other judges of the High Court. It sits in the Four Courts in Dublin and at certain times during the law terms judges leave the Four Courts and go on circuit to sit as the High Court in Cork, Galway,

Kilkenny, Sligo, Ennis, Limerick, Dundalk and Waterford to deal with personal injury actions and appeals from the Circuit Courts in the area.

Any person claiming that legislation is contrary to the Constitution in some respect will commence the action in the High Court. The broad range of business carried out by the court can be gauged from the following list: admiralty, asylum, bail application, bankruptcy, chancery (e.g. injunctions, company liquidations), appeals as well as personal injury actions from the Circuit Court in Dublin and the provinces, common law motions, competition, applications in relation to the dental and medical councils, probate, Solicitors Act, taxation of costs matters, judicial reviews, family law, hepatitis C cases, European arrest warrants, extradition, wards of court and the jury trials. The latter trials concern defamation actions as well as false imprisonment and malicious prosecution in all of which a jury is required.

The type and ever-increasing volume of litigation coming before the High Court is almost endless and constitutes a heavy administrative workload for the President and the Courts Service staff as it does for those judges and staff administering the other courts in the system.

A new division of the court is the **Commercial Court**. As its title suggests it is devoted exclusively to commercial actions with claims of a €1 million or more in each case. Once listed for this court each case is monitored closely as it progresses towards a hearing. This case management results in actions reaching a hearing much sooner than would otherwise be the case. Sitting in court no. 16 the judge or judges who adjudicate in this court take motions each Monday in common with the many other High Courts. All appeals from the High Court go directly to the Supreme Court.

The Central Criminal Court

This is the name given to the court which exercises the criminal power or jurisdiction of the High Court. The judge or judges who sit on this court are High Court judges. It deals with the most serious of crimes, including murder and rape. Trials are conducted to the same formula as the Circuit Criminal Court. It sits in the Four Courts and, occasionally, at provincial centres in order to facilitate witnesses, Gardaí and others appearing before the court. Appeals may be taken to the Court of Criminal Appeal or the Supreme Court.

The Supreme Court

The Supreme Court is comprised of the Chief Justice and eight other judges. The President of the High Court is an *ex-officio* member of the court. The vast bulk of the work handled by the court are appeals from civil actions and motions in the High Court with an occasional appeal coming directly from the Central Criminal Court and Court of Criminal Appeal. As stated earlier, it also deals with consultative cases stated by Circuit Court judges requiring the opinion of the court on a point of law.

From time to time, the court is asked to decide whether a particular Bill, or part of a Bill, sent to the President or *Uachtarán na hÉireann* to be signed into law, is repugnant to the Constitution. This is done under one of the President's few absolute powers given to her under Article 26 of the Constitution. She must first consult with the Council of State but then has sole discretion whether to refer the Bill to the Supreme Court, which hears legal argument for and against the Bill's constitutionality and gives a written judgment not later than 60 days after the date the Bill was referred to the court.

THE LAW TERMS

Law Terms 2006

Hilary sittings: January 11 – April 7.
Easter sittings: April 24 – June 1.
Trinity sittings: June 14 – July 31.
Michaelmas sittings: October 2 – December 21.

Law Terms 2007

Hilary: January 11 – March 30.
Easter: April 16 – May 24.
Trinity: June 6 – July 31.
Michaelmas: October 1 – December 21.

Law Terms 2008

Hilary: January 11 – March 14.
Easter: March 31 – May 8.
Trinity: May 21 – July 31.
Michaelmas: October 6 – December 21.

Law Terms 2009

Hilary: January 11 – April 3.
Easter: April 20 – May 28.
Trinity: June 10 – July 31.
Michaelmas: October 5 – December 31.

During the long vacation each year, from July 31 to the start of the new law year in October, sittings of the High Court are held every two weeks. However, a judge is always available to deal with urgent matters.

CHAPTER 5

Public Relations and the Law of Agency

It is likely that most Public Relations practitioners never address their mind to the legal relationships that *may* exist between them and their client when dealing or contracting on behalf of the client with a third party. One important aspect of that relationship is the law of agency which, in its own right, is a body of law that practitioners and students of the profession should be familiar with in order to fully understand the rights and obligations involved.

Unlike the content of the earlier chapters 1 to 4, the language in this and other chapters that follow will necessarily be more technical but every effort is made to simplify it and to make the legal points and principles as relevant to the Public Relations and corporate communications profession as possible.

The law of agency is very substantial. It applies directly to many relationships in the world of trade and commerce. Its application to the field of Public Relations is narrow but nonetheless valid in certain respects.

In reading what follows practitioners should consider themselves as agents in order to fully understand how this particular law operates in relation to their business dealings on behalf of their clients. They, in turn, should be regarded as principals. Therefore, in order to understand how this law of agency impacts on the practice of Public Relations and corporate communications, one should judge how they fit into any of the situations that follow.

Definitions

According to one of the best legal authorities, "agency" is a comprehensive word used to describe the relationship that arises where one person, called an agent, is appointed to act as representative of another person, called a principal, in any given number of ways. The relationship can come into existence in a number of ways including by express appointment, by the subsequent ratification by the principal of a contract made on his behalf without any authorisation from him and by implication or operation of law in cases where it is urgently necessary that one person should act on behalf of another.

An agent is a person who is employed to bring the principal into contractual relations with a third party. While there are many different types of agents, the category that best describes the relationship into which Public Relations and communication practitioner would most likely fall into is that referred to as general agents. These are agents who have implied authority to enter into any contracts normally within the scope of the profession (trade or business) that the principal has appointed them agents to. The business they are appointed to act in is of a particular kind.

For the purpose of completeness, the other main categories of agent are special agents, such an estate agent appointed for one special task, the sell a property, and universal agents, who have power to enter into any contracts for which the principal has capacity to contract. These are usually appointed by power of attorney.

Power of Attorney

In the ordinary situation, the appointment of an agent need not be in writing for it to be valid. In fact, there is only one situation where it must be in writing and that is where the agent has to execute a deed. This is the category of universal agent explained in the previous paragraph. In such a circumstance, the agent must be given a formal **power of attorney** to do so. This is a deed, a document under seal in which a person is appointed as attorney or agent to carry out a specific act or acts on behalf of a named person – the principal - for a specified period.

The document will contain a clause stating that the person who made the appointment would agree to ratify and confirm everything the attorney or agent did on his or her behalf within the scope of his or her defined powers. The principal as such is bound by every act done by the attorney or agent within the scope of his or her authority.

However, the formality of entering into such a legal document is confined to special circumstances and it is true to say that, usually, an agent acts under less extensive powers than those conferred by a power of attorney. For example, a person wishing to sell a property will instruct an estate agent. That is an agent of a particular type whose business is buying and selling property on behalf of clients, who are his or her principals. The agent is given power or authority to negotiate the sale for a set sum of money. There will be adverse consequences for the agent if the property is sold below the price set by the principal without the principal's consent.

Act in Good Faith

The primary duty of the agent is to act in all good faith towards his or her principal and to give as much care and attention to those duties as to one's own affair, meaning acting *bona fi*des. Almost 130 years ago, it was decided by an English court that an agent must act in good faith at all times and to avoid a conflict of interest which might actually or potentially be detrimental to his principal. Any benefit accruing must be handed to the principal unless he wants the agent to keep it.

If a Public Relations adviser is authorised to carry out a specific task, such as being instructed to inform the public via the media that the client principal is going to build a block of apartments, the adviser is not allowed by the law to delegate that duty. That is a very simple example but nonetheless illustrates the strictness of the authority.

The PR adviser as agent must carry out the duties for which he or she was appointed, in the same way as the estate agent must perform the duty imposed to sell a property or a solicitor to carry out the instructions to execute a conveyance of a property or to administer the estate of a deceased person. The agent must carry out the instructions from the principal within the scope of his or her authority, not to exceed them, not to delegate them and to carry out the duty in the name of the principal or p.p. (meaning *per procurationem*) the principal.

People working in Public Relations and corporate communications are well used to working long hours. In a way, that fits nicely into their role as agents. For example, when an agent is appointed for a *specific* purpose, that work can be carried out in the agent's own time. There are no fixed hours, as most employees have, and, subject to any agreement to the contrary, are left to their own devices as to the manner, method and time period in which to carry the duty out. Of course, agents will bring their own expertise into play in fulfilling the duty because, after all, that is probably the reason they were appointed in the first place.

Scope of Authority

So far, there is nothing to legally worry about in the relationship between the agent and principal. However, legal problems can arise when an agent does some act which is beyond the scope of his or her authority from the principal.

There are common law rules covering this area with case

law or precedent to back them up but the general rule is that it will be the client principal who will be held responsible, or liable at law, for any fraud perpetrated by the agent. For this to be so, the fraud must be committed by the agent acting within his or her actual or implied authority, not otherwise.

Consequently, each such case has to be looked at separately. Each depends on its own set of circumstances. A cynic (or prudent person) might advise that if a principal terminates his relations with an agent, the principal should notify this to all third parties who had dealings with the agent acting on behalf of that principal. This would be to ensure that the principal was relieved of responsibility for the (former) agent's future actions. This is taking an extreme view of the obligation that the law imposes on a prudent professional or business person.

Actual and Ostensible Authority – The Distinction

A contract made by an agent is binding on the principal and the third party with whom the contract was made but only if the agent was acting within the limits of the authority given by the principal. In order to fully understand this it is important to point out that there is a distinction between an agent's *actual* authority on the one hand, and his *apparent* or *ostensible* authority on the other.

The following definitions from the English courts explain what *actual* and *ostensible* authority are in this context:

- An *actual* authority is a legal relationship between principal and agent created by a consensual agreement to which they alone are parties. Its scope is to be ascertained by applying ordinary principles of constructions of contracts, including any proper implications from the express words used, the usages of trade or the course of business between the parties. Actual authority may be express or implied.

- *Ostensible* or apparent authority is the authority of the agent as it *appears* to others.

The type of issue or problem that can be thrown up in this form of relationship is illustrated by what happens when an estate agent is employed to sell a house or apartment and whether the agent has *implied* authority to accept a deposit from a prospective purchaser. If the agent accepts the money as stakeholder before the contract is signed but then misappropriates the money in some way or becomes insolvent, what is the situation regarding the vendor and the purchaser with regard to the deposit? The authorities support the claim of the purchaser.

The court has ruled that the taking of a deposit is reasonably incidental to the functions of an estate agent and, consequently, the agent holds the money throughout the pre-contract period because of his agency. Therefore, the principal is responsible for what results from the exercise by the agent of his *implied* authority. However, an agent who exceeds his apparent authority will generally have no liability to his or her principal since the principal cannot be bound by the unauthorised contracts made for him. The agent will be responsible and therefore liable in such a case to the third parties for breach of authority or warranty.

Agent's Duties

There is a contractual relationship between the client principal and the PR agent. When the agent agrees to perform services for his or her principal for reward, there is a contract between them which imposes rights and obligations on both sides. This is so even if the agent undertakes his duties without reward – the agent still has obligations to the principal. These include carrying out the task that was agreed between them.

An agent is entitled to be repaid his expenses and to be

indemnified by the principal against losses and liabilities when properly doing any work within the limit of his authority. However, should he act negligently or without authorisation, he forfeits this entitlement. Agents are entitled to be paid whatever remuneration for services is agreed with the principal. If the amount of the remuneration was not agreed, then the agent must receive a sum considered reasonable in the circumstances.

Ending an Agency

There are two ways in which an agency is ended: by act of the parties and by operation of law. It is determined by act of the parties if there is mutual agreement to that effect, or if the agent's authority is renounced by him or her or revoked by the principal. However, in the latter situation, care and professional advice needs to be taken to ensure either party does not leave himself or herself open to be sued for breach of contract. When it is ended by operation of law, it can be brought about by the occurrence of some event which makes the agency unlawful and also by death, insanity or bankruptcy of either the agent or the principal.

Injunction

An individual may apply to the High Court for an order called an injunction for any number of reasons including, for example, compelling another individual not to dissipate his assets below the level of a sum due to the plaintiff, or to compel another party to supply him with goods allegedly agreed under an agency or distribution agreement, the court will decide whether the injunction should be granted only after examining the facts and circumstances of the case under the following three principles:

- Is there a serious issue to be tried between the parties in the main substantive action between them?
- Would an award of damages be an adequate remedy (instead of granting an injunction)?
- Whether the balance of convenience favoured the granting rather than refusing to grant the injunction?

If the court decides, for example, that damages were an adequate remedy in the main action for the party seeking the injunction, it will not grant the injunction. In those circumstances the case will take its normal course and come to hearing when the plaintiff will seek to win his case and be awarded damages to compensate him for whatever loss the courts finds he suffered.

There is a case precedent for this last example in which the Supreme Court also ruled that where there was an implied or oral agency agreement, that agreement would be terminable upon reasonable notice. That period would not be in excess of six months.

Summary

The common law of agency is a body of law that applies to a consensual relationship in which one person – an agent – agrees or consents to act on behalf of another person – the principal – and subject to the principal's control.

In relation to acting as an agent, the law would hold that a practitioner acts in the capacity as a *trustee* for their client in several business situations where trust and confidence are imposed, thereby giving rise to another heavy legal responsibility carried by practitioners. As such, the law would impress practitioners with the obligation of acting honestly and diligently and being legally accountable for any breach of that trust.

CHAPTER 6

Companies and Partnerships

When two or more people get together to conduct a particular business and to make profits for themselves, they either form a partnership or register a company. In the case of setting up a Public Relations or corporate communications business they usually decide that a registered company, rather than a partnership, is the best option. There are very good reasons for this, not least because the business may be risky at the outset and the promoters will want to protect themselves from having to pay any liabilities or debts that may result if the business proves unsuccessful.

Unlike a partnership, a limited liability company is a legal entity brought into existence under ancient laws which define its limits and rights. It is brought into existence by registration and it is dissolved by a procedure, known as winding up or liquidation, when it becomes insolvent and unable to pay its debts, in much the same way as a business person is adjudicated a bankrupt if his or her business fails.

When a company becomes insolvent, it may be wound up but its owners will remain untouched by the claims of the creditors owed money by the company unless, of course, they can prove to the High Court that the business was conducted as a fraud on its creditors or that it continued to trade knowing that it was insolvent. Either of these situations could have far-reaching consequences for them, as we shall see later in this chapter.

Advantages of a Limited Liability Company

Most companies are registered as limited liability companies, which means that the shareholders of those companies have limited their liability or exposure. If such a company fails, the shareholders' liability is limited to the amount, if any, remaining unpaid on the shares held by them. This contrasts sharply with a firm run as a partnership in which the partners are individually and equally responsible for the debts incurred by the firm. Likewise, in the case of a sole trader, his or her business is their property and obligations and debts of the businesses become the person's own personal liabilities.

There are other advantages also in forming a company instead of a partnership or a sole trader, not least because it is easier for the company to borrow money and have it secured against its assets. If a partner dies, it could result in the partnership being dissolved while the death of a sole trader sounds the death knell for the business. However, there is no such problem or disruption for a company in the event of the death or retirement of one of the main shareholders or, indeed, the principal shareholder. There will just usually be a change of ownership of that person's shareholding.

Prudent management of a PR or communications business would, therefore, unquestionably dictate that the promoters of the business should set about forming a company rather than a partnership.

Salomon versus Salomon

Apart from limiting their liability promoters of new companies also bring about a separate legal personality so that the failure of their incorporated business will not automatically make them bankrupt. Therefore, we can say with legal certainty that a company has a separate legal entity from its members.

The basis of this certainty is the watershed case of *Salomon v. Salomon & Co.*, first reported in the 1897 from the highest court in England, the House of Lords. The case concerned the distribution of assets among the creditors of a boot manufacturing company that had failed during the recession four years earlier. The essential ruling was that a company had a separate legal entity from that of its members. Therefore, Mr. Salomon the first plaintiff, was not liable for the company's debts. The court unanimously ruled that since, legally, a company was wholly distinct from its shareholders, priority had to be given to the *debenture* (a set amount of money loaned to the company and secured on its assets) held by Mr. Salomon in the sum of £10,000 over and above the £7,500 owed to secured creditors.

Lord Macnaghten, referring to a what has since become section 18(2) of the (Irish) Companies Act 1963, said the company was at law a different person from its shareholders. The company was not in law the agent of the shareholders or trustee for them. Neither were the shareholders as members liable except to the extent and in the manner provided by the Companies Act.

However, in a situation where a company fails today and the owners of the company had earlier personally guaranteed the debts of the company, they will become liable and could be adjudicated bankrupt as a consequence. Therefore, having regard to the foregoing, there is no question but that PR firms should be registered limited liability companies. The company is registered under the Companies Acts 1963 to 2005 in the Companies Registration Office situated at Parnell House, 14 Parnell Square, Dublin 1 (Tel no. 01–8045200; www.cro.ie). It becomes a body corporate as and from the date mentioned in its certificate of incorporation. It then has a separate legal personality.

Directors

The persons who direct the policy of a company are called "directors" and the people who nominate the directors are those who subscribe to the company's capital by purchasing shares. This is usually subscribed by a small number of shareholders who decide to undertake and operate a Public Relations or communications' business for this purpose. Being a separate legal entity from those who run it, only the company can be sued for its obligations and can sue in its own name to enforce its right. When the original shareholders meet, they appoint the directors who then conduct the business operations of the company.

The company cannot be managed in any willy-nilly fashion. It has to have purpose. How it is governed depends on the purpose or purposes set out in the *articles of association* adopted originally by the members when establishing the particular company. The members allocate most of the decision-making of the company to the board of directors of which there must be legally at least two. The company must also have a secretary, who is assigned responsibility by companies' legislation for its administrative and legal affairs, as well as a professionally qualified auditor appointed (or re-appointed) at the annual general meetings of the shareholders each year.

Companies Registration Office

Among the functions carried out by the Companies Registration Office (CRO) – which has statutory authority - are the incorporation of companies and the registration of business names. It also enforces the companies' legislation with regard to the filing obligations of companies.

Business name

When a registered company carries on a business other than under the full corporate name, that business name must be registered in the Companies Registration Office (CRO). This is a legal requirement which binds a partnership and an individual as much as it does a registered company. If a partnership is carrying on business other than under the true surname of the partners, it must register the name it is using. Similarly, any individual trading under a name other than his or her true surname is obliged to register that name. The legislation which imposes these obligations is the Registration of Business Names Act 1963 (its English equivalent is the Registration of Business Names Act 1916).

Protection for Creditors

One particular safeguard that exists for creditors of a company is the legal obligation imposed on every company to file at least once in every calendar year an annual return to the CRO. The information is supplied in a document known as Form B1. Each registered company had its own annual return date, known as its ARD but since May 17, 2004, if a company has its annual return ready early in a particular year, it may make the return up to a current date and file it, and also inform the CRO on the new Form B1 that it wants to keep its ARD for the following year.

Companies who fail to comply with this statutory obligation can be struck off the register of companies. The directors of such companies can also be prosecuted. If a company is struck off, the directors and other main shareholders lose the very protection they sought when forming the company in the first place, that of their limited liability which then no longer exists. As a consequence, these persons can be held personally liable for the debts incurred after the company was struck from the register.

According to the CRO, the assets of such companies then become the property of the State. Companies that are struck off may usually be reinstated on the register but this can be an expensive process, involving legal and other costs. There is a high level of vigilance by the CRO that has resulted in many thousands of companies being struck off in recent years.

Non-compliance with provisions in the Companies Acts is a criminal offence. Concerns about corporate malpractice led to the enactment of the Company Law Enforcement Act in 2001 and the creation of the office of the Director of Corporate Enforcement (ODCE). Encouraging compliance with company law and investigating and enforcing suspected breaches of the legislation are listed among the Office's main functions. Their website is www.odce.ie.

In January, 2006, the Director secured his Office's first court conviction under section 243(1) of the Companies Act 1990, which prohibits the falsification of a book or document relating to the property or affairs of a company.

An individual who was both director and secretary of a company pleaded guilty to falsifying the company's financial statement which had been presented to a bank along with another document in order to have its overdraft facility renewed. The documents represented that the financial statements had been audited by a named firm of chartered accountants. However, the company was not a client of the audit firm, which denied the authenticity of the documents presented to the bank. The director was fined €500 and ordered to pay €300 costs. Subsequently, the Director of Corporate Enforcement, Mr Paul Appleby, stated:

> "We were particularly anxious in this case to uphold the integrity of audited financial statements. An auditor's opinion provides valuable independent assurance for the public at large of the state of affairs of the company. We

> cannot tolerate a director representing a set of financial statements as having been audited by a recognised firm of auditors when this was not the case."

Registered Office

Every company is obliged by legislation to have an office, known as a Registered Office. This is the seat of the company and the importance attached to this requirement is the fact that all legal and other documents will officially be served on the company at this office.

Winding-up

There are a number of ways in which a company may be wound-up – by the members of the company themselves in what's termed a voluntary winding up, secondly, by the creditors of the company in a similarly termed voluntary winding-up and thirdly, by the High Court in a compulsory winding-up. Voluntary liquidations are much less expensive and quicker than court winding ups. The appointed of a chartered accountant who is specialist in liquidations is common to all three forms of winding-up. The liquidator's function is to wind up the affairs and distribute the assets of the company.

Sole Traders

As the name suggests, a sole trader is a single individual running a business on his or her own, either in their own name or with a name registered under the Registration of Business Names Act 1963 (mentioned above). There are few restrictions against anybody setting up as a sole trader as there is no necessity to have formal qualifications. Registration with the Revenue authorities for the payment of Value Added Tax (VAT) and related purposes must be complied with in order to trade.

Partnerships

Partnerships are governed by the Partnership Act 1890 which defines a partnership as "the relation which subsists between persons carrying on a business in common with a view to profit," other than registered or otherwise incorporated bodies.

Where any two or more persons agree to engage in a common business, they automatically constitute a partnership and no formality is required. There are limits to the number of persons who can combine together to form a partnership.

Advice

This chapter has merely touched on the various relationships highlighted. It does not purport to offer advice. Anybody wishing to know more or to become involved with or to form one of the relationships should consult a specialist in the field, such as a chartered accountant or a solicitor.

Chapter 7

Legal Obligations in Taking Care of Client Needs

A Public Relations practitioner commissioned by a client to fulfil a particular function within the expertise of the practitioner is legally bound to perform that task to a standard. If that standard is breached and it results in loss to the client, economic or otherwise, the question that arises is whether the client can sue the practitioner. There are a number of possible heads under which such an action could be taken against the PR practitioner including breach of trust referred to in Chapter 5. They involve a consideration of the respective laws of negligence and contract.

Negligence

Negligence is part of a body of law known as tort that is a civil wrong. It is a civil (not criminal) wrong and is best understood if it is applied to three different scenarios: firstly, to a road traffic accident in which the driver of a car was negligent in not keeping a proper look-out and collided with another car, causing personal injury to himself and his passenger. The driver's passenger was also negligent by not wearing a seat belt.

Therefore, if the case goes to court, the driver will be held by the judge to be negligent and his passenger will be held to be guilty of contributory negligence. As a result, the injured passenger will get at least 20% less damages than would otherwise be the case. Secondly, if a surgeon carries out a medical procedure on a patient and is found by a court to have done so negligently as a consequence of carrying out the procedure in a substandard way, the patient will be awarded damages for medical negligence because the surgeon did not treat the patient properly and, thirdly, if a solicitor fails to conduct any, or any proper, searches of the planning registries to ascertain if a public highway is going to be built through a property being purchased by his client.

Essential Elements

There are a number of elements to be understood when dissecting the civil wrong of negligence in relation to the practice of a Public Relations practitioner or advisor. (Advisor to a client may be the most particularly appropriate context in which to examine the relationship because it could be in this context that the PR person was negligent in offering, or not offering, expert or competent advice to a client):

- The existence of a duty of care by the PR person to the client – duty of care being a legally recognised obligation requiring the practitioner/adviser to conform to a certain standard of behaviour for the protection of the client against unreasonable risks.
- That the practitioner/adviser was in breach of that standard or duty care.
- That the breach caused the client to suffer some injury, loss or damage as a result.
- That the amount of the loss is recoverable in law.

Duty of Care

Whether the law recognises that a PR practitioner or adviser owes a duty of care to the client must be established to the court's satisfaction by the plaintiff client. That onus or burden must be proved on the balance of probabilities. It is legally well established that a doctor owes a duty of care to his or her patient and that duty extends to many aspects of the patient's care including diagnosis, treatment and advice.

Equally, it has been decided that a local authority whose inspector passed fit the foundations of a house later found to have been built on the unstable foundation of a rubbish tip was liable. The professional person owed a duty of care, not only to the then owner but to all subsequent owners who might suffer injury or loss as a result.

Each case that is taken in which a plaintiff seeks to establish negligence on the part of a particular party is judged on its own circumstances. Negligence may be claimed arising out of doing or saying something or failing to do or say something, in other words by act or omission. But in deciding whether to impose liability or fault on the party against whom the claim of negligence is made, the court will have regard to what's known in law as the "**neighbour principle**."

This principle first emerged from a case worth citing here because of its importance, *Donoghue v. Stevenson* which was decided by the English House of Lords in the early 1930s. Lord Atkin said:

> "The rule that you are to love your neighbour becomes in law you must not injure your neighbour; and the lawyer's question, who is my neighbour? receives a restricted reply. You must take reasonable care to avoid acts or omissions which you can reasonably foresee would be liable to injury your neighbour. Who, then, in law, is my neighbour? The answer seems to be – persons who are so closely and directly affected by my act that I ought reasonably to have them in contemplation as being so affected when I am directing my mind to the acts or omissions which are called in question."

Therefore, were a client to take a legal action, the first hill that must be climbed is for the client to prove on the balance of probabilities that the PR practitioner owed him a duty of care. Each case is decided on its own merits.

If the clients succeed in this, the next issue which must be established by the client is whether the PR practitioner breached that duty of care; that is whether the practitioner was in breach of the appropriate standard of care that the law would probably impose, that he or she failed to possess the skill required by his or her profession to perform the particular duty or neglected to use the skill he or she possessed. The courts would have regard to the practice of other practitioners of similar status in the same field or profession.

Having overcome these obstacles, the client must prove he suffered damage or loss of some kind as a result of the practitioner's breach of his duty of care. That damage or loss must be proved to have been sufficiently closely related to the act of negligence itself. In seeking to resolve this question, the court will try and establish whether the harm that occurred was *reasonably foreseeable.* This is another crucial hurdle that the client must surmount.

The test

In determining remoteness of damage the test which the courts apply is the "foreseeability" test, that is whether the damage or injury was of such a kind as the reasonable person should have foreseen and that such foreseeability must be of the damage which, in fact, happened. In short, the test is whether the damage was of such a kind as a reasonable person should have foreseen.

There is a range of defences that a person sued in tort can mount but which one or ones used will depend on the nature and circumstances of the particular claim. However, there will be a general denial in which the claim will be totally refuted. In the case of a traffic accident, for example, the defendant denies that the accident happened as alleged or at all and even if it did happen (which is denied), the defendant will plead that he was not guilty of the alleged or any negligence. It may also be part of the defence strategy to plead that the plaintiff (the PR practitioner's client for example) was guilty of contributory negligence. If the court holds the latter, then the practitioner's liability may be substantially reduced, depending on the view taken of the evidence by the judge.

People not familiar with the law find it extraordinary that the law allows a defendant in a claim such as that under discussion to totally deny that an event such as a traffic accident happened or that a botched medical procedure arising from a hugely traumatic claim for alleged medical negligence even occurred. However, the reason for this is that unless the claim is denied, the defendant is taken to admit it. Unless the tortuous event is denied, the defendant would be "shooting himself in the foot" by restricting his defence to a pure assessment of damages only. He could not fight the case on liability.

Damages

Whether a client brings an action under the law of contract or tort, the usual remedy sought is an award of damages. This may be quantified as a sum for general damages in addition to a sum for special damages, generally referred to as "specials", which, in the case of a plaintiff who was unable to return to work as a result of some negligent act by the defendant, would include a sum representing lost wages.

Summary

Generally, if a professional such a PR practitioner, acts in accordance with the general and approved practice of his or her profession, they cannot be held negligent, except, perhaps, in some very exceptional circumstances. However, the corollary is true. If such a professional fails to follow the general and approved practice of the profession, without good cogent reason, it is likely he or she will be held negligent.

Contract

A client suing his or her Public Relations practitioner would most likely be legally advised to bring the action in contract as well as in tort. This would be done on the basis that a contractual relationship had existed between both parties in the first place. But that has to be proved to be a contract for service, such as would be the reality of the contractual relationship between a PR practitioner and client.

Whether principles of contract law govern the case is a matter of law and fact for determination by the judge hearing the particular action? Although such claims based on contract are not common, there is a piece of legislation that a client could avail of to mount a claim for breach of contract against a practitioner and that is the Sale of Goods and Supply of Services Act 1980 which repealed the much older legislation common to Ireland and England, the Sale of Goods Act 1893.

Although the 1980 Act is mainly used in terms of the purchase and supply of goods, it also regulates to a certain extent the provision of services by including or implying certain warranties (terms) in a contract.

For the purpose of clarification, a "warranty" is a term ancillary to the main purposes of a contract which entitles the consumer client to a claim for damages should the supplier of the service breach it. The definition section of the Act defines "business" as including "profession."

The Sale of Goods and Supply of Services Act 1980 provides that the supplier of services warrants that:

- he has the necessary skill to render the services, and
- that he will supply the service with due skill, care and diligence.

These are implied terms as to the quality of the service to be provided and are similar to those that the common law would have implied into such contracts prior to 1980. It is always possible that terms such as these could be excluded by the agreement of the parties before the contract was entered into (as provided for in section 40 of the 1980 Act). The Act provides that where the recipient (client) of the service is a consumer the exclusion must be shown by the supplier of the service to be fair and reasonable and, in addition, to have been brought to the consumer's (client) attention.

Contract Generally

The law of contract is a huge body of law, which would deserve an entire chapter, at least, in order to reasonably explain the various parts and strands that go to make it up. Suffice here to define it as a legal term which describes an agreement between two or more persons to do or not to do a particular thing. It is an agreement or covenant between two or more people in which each binds himself or herself to do or refrain from doing some act, and each acquires a right to what the other promises.

Not every agreement is a contract. If John asks Mary out to dinner and Mary accepts, this is not a contract although it is an agreement. However, it was never intended by the parties that John would be entitled to claim damages if Mary failed to turn up at the restaurant. The agreement is not enforceable at law, something that is an essential element of a contract that creates rights and obligations. Barristers cannot sue their instructing solicitor and client for payment of their fees so, therefore, any contracts they made for payment of their fees are unenforceable by them. However, solicitors can (and do) sue clients for their fees.

The vital ingredient of an enforceable contract is the *intention* of the parties. A person entering into a contract should intend that he should be bound by the rights that the contract creates. There are two factors that must be in every contract:

1. an agreement consisting of a communicated offer and acceptance between the parties to the contract, and
2. consideration, meaning that before the contract becomes enforceable each party must obtain consideration for the promises that he or she made.

Both parties must receive a benefit. Applying this to the circumstances of this book, it is safe to say the usual consideration a PR practitioner receives to fulfil his or her part of the bargain is monetary!

Although most contracts in which consideration is present are binding whether they are made verbally, in writing or by implication or by a combination of all three forms, there are certain contracts which the law says shall not be binding unless they are made in a particular form, either under seal, *i.e.* by deed, or in writing.

There are a large number of contracts that are not enforceable unless they are made in writing but the one that the general public would most identify with is a contract for the sale of lands or interest in lands, e.g. a house or apartment. The others are not really relevant to the topic under consideration in this chapter.

CHAPTER 8

Privacy and Confidentiality

At some stage while engaged in representing a client a Public Relations practitioner will have interaction in some possible respect with the privacy laws. Respect for the privacy rights of others and of safeguarding the confidences of a practitioner's present (and former employer, if appropriate) employer is not just a rule of conduct for all practitioners but are aspects of the law which must be observed. Without stretching the imagination too far, this could arise in the context of seeking private or personal information on behalf of a client and in moving from one employer to another where inherent or external pressure could be brought to bear to disclose information about former clients and or of the PR firm itself.

The somewhat nebulous concept of the right to privacy has become a public talking point in recent years due to the increasing intrusion by the media in an aggressive media market into the private lives of citizens, some of whom are in the public life and some who are not. This was identified as a justification for the establishment of a press council that would provide an alternative means of redress to going to court by members of the public aggrieved by something published about them in the press. A discussion about privacy, as here, might be criticised for being unduly academic but to do otherwise would fail to do justice to a topic that affects all of us fundamentally.

Strange as it may seem, the common law no more recognises the existence of a right to privacy than it does the right of a journalist to protect his or her confidential sources of information. There is no general right to privacy in Ireland.

This may seem strange in a common law country like Ireland whose fundamental law, the Constitution or *Bunreacht na hÉireann,* also fails to *expressly* guarantee a right to privacy. There are two references to the word "private' in the Constitution. These are private enterprise and private property but there is no reference to a general right to privacy being recognised or guaranteed. However, through the development of our case law since 1937, the superior courts imply recognition of such a right - but only in a certain context -in the Constitution. Simply put, they read the right into it. It is referred to by judges and lawyers as an unenumerated right but it is no less a right for this than others that can be read in the Constitution, rights such as the right to life, the right to freedom of expression, press freedom, the right to bodily integrity and some others.

A person's right to privacy relating to their personal records is protected by a number of pieces of legislation, including the Data Protection (Amendment) Act 2003 and the Freedom of Information Act 1997, as amended, which will be considered in Chapter 13.

Claims that their right to privacy has been breached and asking the courts for protection have become more frequent. Two examples: a member of the U2 rock band, David Evans, otherwise known as The Edge, together with his wife, went to the High Court in 2005 for an order to stop a tabloid newspaper from publishing details of a family member's illness. On January 15, 2006, the High Court dismissed a claim by a Dublin solicitor that his right to privacy was breached by the Mahon Tribunal's decision to publicly inquire into a number of land deals in which he was allegedly involved with other named persons and his attendance at the public hearings would reveal his confidential business affairs. He claimed this breached his rights to privacy under the Constitution and the European Convention on Human Rights.

Rejecting the claim the judge outlined the well-established recognition of a constitutional right to privacy but he emphasised that it was not an unqualified right. The constitutional right to privacy could be "encroached upon" in the interests of the common good, subject to the requirements of constitutional justice and fair procedures.

Landmark Case

Nobody needs a lawyer or a weighty legal tome to define what "privacy" is. A dictionary definition of "privacy" is "the state of being private and undisturbed … a person's right to this … freedom of intrusion or public attention … avoidance of publicity." Another definition which has its origins in a text written in the late 19th century in the US: "The right to be let alone."

In fact, this latter simple definition was adopted with approval by the President of the High Court in this country in one of the few cases in which breach of privacy was the central issue, that taken by two journalists, Geraldine Kennedy (current Editor of the *Irish Times)* and Bruce Arnold (a noted columnist with the *Irish Independent*), in the mid-1980s. They brought their claim for damages against the State arising out of the clandestine interception of telephone conversations by order of the then Minister for Justice, reportedly to try and identify the person or persons allegedly leaking Cabinet information to them. What the judge said in ruling in their favour and awarding them damages is important in the context of an examination of a right not mentioned in the Constitution but now being read into it:

> "Though not specifically guaranteed by the Constitution, the right of privacy is one of the fundamental personal rights of the citizen which flows from the Christian and democratic nature of the State. It is not an unqualified right. Its exercise may be restricted by the constitutional

> right of others, by the requirements of the common good, and it is subject to the requirements of public order and morality. The action of the Executive in 'tapping' the telephones of two journalists without any lawful authority, and in interfering with and intruding upon the privacy of the journalists in question, constituted an attack on their dignity and freedom as individuals and as journalists."

(This case led to the enactment of legislation governing telephone interception, the Interception of Postal Packets and Telecommunications Messages (Regulation) Act 1993).

Earlier privacy Cases

The first case in which "privacy" was one of the central issues was decided about 13 years previously. That concerned a young mother of four children from north County Dublin who was threatened with a stroke if she became pregnant again. She and her husband decided to limit their family in accordance with medical advice but in order to do this they needed to import contraceptives (something that was banned by legislation) as there was no availability to contraceptives in this country in the early 1970s. Their efforts to do this failed when the contraceptives were impounded by customs. The woman brought an action challenging the constitutionality of that provision in the legislation – the Customs Consolidation Act – but this was rejected by the High Court. Her appeal to the Supreme Court succeeded and *McGee v. Attorney General* became a watershed decision.

The central theme of the case was the claim by Mrs McGee that the State had no right to interfere in the private life of herself and her husband. By a majority, the court adopted the ruling of the US Supreme Court that the State cannot act as a policeman in the bedroom. Notably, the *McGee* case established the **right to marital privacy** in Ireland, which the State was obliged to protect.

However, in dismissing an appeal in another case subsequently, *Norris v. Attorney General*, the Supreme Court ruled that the right to privacy was not absolute because the State had an interest in the moral character of society. Homosexual acts between consenting male adults in private would not be included within the scope of such privacy, a decision subsequently overturned by the European Court of Human Rights following on its earlier decision in the *Dudgeon v. UK* case in 1981.

European Dimension

Decisions of the European Court and the European Convention on Human Rights, while not binding on Irish courts, must be considered by judges in cases coming before them. The Convention sets out a minimum statement of rights to be protected in this country, and in each State that has signed up to it. It provides a mechanism to allow individuals to enforce it against the State in situations where the State has infringed their rights under the Convention and domestic law has failed to provide a remedy. One of the rights that would seem to be most under threat is the right to respect for private and family life. This is contained in article 8 of the Convention. Both the *Norris* and *Dudgeon* cases were ruled on the basis of article 8 which states:

> "(1) Everyone has the right to respect for his private and family life, his home and his correspondence.
>
> (2) There shall be no interference by a public authority with the exercise of this right

> except such as in accordance with the law and is necessary in a democratic society in the interests of national security, public safety or the economic well-being of the country, for the prevention of disorder or crime, for the protection of health or morals, or for the protection of the rights and freedoms of others."

Concept becoming Clearer

The concept of privacy is becoming clearer with each new case that is the subject of a judicial decision but it still defies precise definition in law. Where does one draw the line in terms of public acts in private places or private acts in public places?

In 1988, the US Supreme Court ruled that citizens could have no reasonable expectation of privacy in items they discarded in the dustbin for the express purpose of having strangers take it away. Therefore the question arises for consideration in Ireland: if unscrupulous individuals go through people's dustbins and discarded rubbish in order to get names and addresses and other information in order to compile lists for use for mail shots or some nefarious use, that does not constitute a breach of privacy or confidentiality? Depending on the use that's made of the information, it is at least arguable that the law has developed to such an extent in Europe that it is.

Article 8 will continue to become more and more important in the context of the development of "privacy" in its many aspects in our own domestic law. One of the effects of the Human Rights Act 2003 (HRA) is that it gives judges an opportunity to interpret the European Convention on Human Rights in a domestic context.

The Convention is, in fact, included as a schedule to the

Irish legislation. For example, the right to privacy in public was considered relatively weak. That is until a recent decision of the European Court in a case involving Princess Caroline, daughter of late Princess Grace of Monaco, brought under her married name in *Von Hanover v. Germany*. She took three magazines to court in Germany after they published articles about her and photographs of her skiing, playing tennis, leaving a restaurant and shopping with her family –all in public places. The courts rejected her claim, ruling that while she was a public person *par excellence*, she was, effectively, "fair game' once she was photographed in public places. The Princess then sued Germany in the European Court, claiming there was a lack of adequate protection for her private life and her image under German law. She won in Strasbourg. The court's ruling in June 2004, dealt with the controversial debate concerning the balancing of the twin guarantees in the European Convention of freedom of expression (press freedom) and for private life in a situation where these rights come into conflict.

Finding that there was a breach by Germany of article 8 of the European Convention on Human Rights, the majority judgment stated:

> "The decisive factor in balancing protection of private life against freedom of expression should lie in the contribution that the published photos and articles make to a debate of general interest. It is clear in the instant case that they made no such contribution since the applicant exercises no official function and the photos and articles related exclusively to details of her private life.
>
> Furthermore, the court considers that the public does not have a legitimate interest in knowing where the applicant is and how she behaves generally in her private life even if she appears in places that cannot always be described

> as secluded and despite the fact that she is well known to the public.
>
> Even if such a public interest exists, as does a commercial interest in the magazines in publishing these photos and these articles, in the instant case those interests must, in the court's view, yield to the applicant's right to the effective protection of her private life."

This decision will have a profound effect in the years ahead on Ireland's developing privacy and defamation laws.

Confidence

The common law right to confidentiality, mentioned at the outset, is a related right recognised by the law. It arose in a number of recent cases, both in Ireland and abroad. The majority Supreme Court judgment in *National Irish Bank v. Radio Telefís Éireann* in 1998 stated:

> "There is no doubt but that there exists a duty and a right of confidentiality between banker and customer and it also exists in many other relationships such as for example doctor and patient and lawyer and client. This duty of confidentiality extends to third parties into whose hands confidential information may come and such third parties can be injuncted to prohibit the disclosure of such confidential information. There is a public interest in the maintenance of such confidentiality for the benefit of society at large."

In the UK in 2001, in the well publicised case of *Douglas v. Hello*! which involved the taking of photographs at the wedding of Catherine Zeta Jones and Michael Douglas, the judge said that privacy extended to those who simply found themselves subjected to an unwarranted intrusion in their private lives. The law no longer needed to construct an artificial relationship of confidentiality between intruder and victim: it could recognise privacy itself as a legal principle drawn from the fundamental value of personal autonomy. The case cantered on a dispute as to whether *OK*! magazine had exclusive rights to the publication of wedding photos which came into the possession of its rival, *Hello*!

Other well-known personalities, such as model, Naomi Campbell, have also gone to the English courts to protect their privacy. In most, if not all of the case, the courts have placed strong reliance on the European Court's rulings with respect to freedom of expression and privacy. Without going into any detail about the facts of the case itself, some commentators have interpreted the House of Lords' decision in the Campbell case as establishing a new civil wrong of privacy but this is far from certain. In any event, while such a decision is not binding on the courts in Ireland, it should be noted that the courts in France recognised a general right to privacy over 100 years ago.

Other Remedies

There are other aspect to the privacy laws that practitioners and students should be aware of in Ireland. That is the existence of two other torts or civil wrongs which members of the public, whether they are celebrities or not, can avail of in order to stop intrusion by the media into their private lives. These are **Trespass** and **Nuisance**.

A person can apply to court for an injunction to stop what is perceived as a trespass to their person or physical property or, indeed, to stop causing a nuisance. Under either or both of these heads, the option of claiming damages is also open to the person. However, there is also a criminal sanction available for breach of privacy.

A person can make a complaint to an Garda Síochána who are empowered, under the Non-Fatal Offences Against the Person Act 1997, to bring a prosecution for **harassment**. Section 10 of the Act states, in part:

> "Any person who, without lawful authority or reasonable excuse, by any means including by use of the telephone, harasses another by persistently following, watching, pestering, besetting or communicating with him or her, shall be guilty of an offence."

It defines "**harass'** as: where he or she, by his or her acts intentionally or recklessly, seriously interferes with the other's peace and privacy or causes alarm, distress or harm to the other person, and the acts are such that a reasonable person would realise that the acts would seriously interfere with the other person's peace and privacy or cause alarm, distress or harm to the other person. A person found guilty by the District Court of this offence could be fined a maximum of €1,900 or 12 months in prison, or both, while the same conviction in the Circuit Court attracts an indeterminate fine and a maximum prison term of seven years.

Privacy Bill 2006

Since all of the above chapter was written, the Privacy Bill 2006 was published on the July 4, 2006 and it is reproduced in its entirety in this book (see Appendix 6).

The purpose of the Bill is to provide for a new tort (a civil wrong) of *violation of privacy*, taking into account the jurisprudence of this country's superior courts and that of the European Court of Human Rights. The Government is not proposing to create a new right in the draft legislation; rather is it seeking to provide a statutory framework in regard to how alleged violations might be dealt with. Although the Bill does not define "privacy," it provides that it is a tort for a person wilfully and without lawful authority to violate the privacy of an individual.

According to the Bill, a person's entitlement to privacy is that which might be reasonable in all the circumstances having regard to the rights of others and to public order and the common good. It goes on to spell this out in more detail. A person's privacy is violated by:

- Subjecting another person to surveillance and by the disclosure of information so obtained;
- the unauthorised use of name, voice or likeness of an individual for commercial purpose;
- the disclosure of personal information or documents of a person; or
- committing an act of harassment, as described in section 10 of the Non-Fatal Offences Against the Persons Act, 1997 Act" (see above).

The Bill sets out a number of defences to a privacy action. The defendant would have to prove that the act in respect of which the action was brought:

- Was done for the purpose of lawfully defending or protecting a person or property (including the prosecution or defence of proceedings either civil or criminal).
- Was authorised or required by law or by a court or process of a court established by law.
- Was done by a public servant:
  - (i) acting in the course if his or her duties, or
  - (ii) in circumstances where he or she had

reasonable grounds for believing that he or she was acting in the course of his or her duties.

- Consisted of the installation or operation, in good faith, of a closed circuit television or other surveillance system –
  - (i) for a purpose authorised by law, or
  - (ii) for the purpose of detecting or preventing the commission of an offences or for the protection of persons or property.
- Was an act of newsgathering, provided any disclosure of material obtained as a result of such act was done in good faith for the purpose of discussing a subject of public importance for the public benefit and fair and reasonable in all the circumstances.

A few other points worth noting in this brief look at the proposed legislation is that claims may be taken in either the Circuit or High Court (non-jury); if it is taken in the former, the court will be empowered to grant total damages of €50,000. The courts will also be empowered to hear all or part of the hearing in private. Claims must be taken within one year from the discovery of the alleged acts, although a court may extend this period to two years. However, an individual will not be allowed to take a privacy action unless they notify in writing the person they intend to sue within three months from the date that the alleged cause of action arose, although the court can waive compliance with this stipulation. The Bill applies to all types of media, including not only print and broadcast, but on the internet or by any means now possible with the advance of technology.

Widespread opposition to the Bill was voiced immediately after its publication by many sections of the print media. They argued that such claims of violation of privacy should more properly be handled by the office of the proposed Press Ombudsman and the Press Council of Ireland whose draft

Code of Practice specifically demands respect for the privacy and sensibilities of individuals. However, it also states that the right to privacy should not prevent publication of matters of public record or in the public interest.

Unlike the draft Defamation Bill 2006, the person taking a privacy action is *not* required to file an affidavit (sworn statement) verifying the assertions or allegations they pleaded in the grounding court documents (e.g. a Circuit Court civil bill, High Court plenary summons or statement of claim). If claimants were obliged by the proposed privacy legislation to file such an affidavit, it could reduce or eliminate spurious or frivolous claims especially with a sanction of criminal prosecution for people who making false or misleading claims in their affidavit.

Chapter 9

Libel and Malicious Falsehood: Traps for the Unwary

Risk Management

Should PR firms ask their clients for an indemnity against the possibility of being sued for libel in situations where press releases issued on behalf of those clients contain material that could be considered problematic by being contentious, critical, or, in general terms, risky copy?

This is a question that ought to be foremost in the minds of account executives when preparing copy for submission to the media for publication. Should they get their clients to sign-off the material before it is e-mailed, faxed, posted or couriered to newspaper officers, radio or TV stations at which stage the copy is no longer under the control of the PR, public affairs, advertising or other practitioner? It may come as a surprise for people to know that some practitioners very prudently do get their clients to sign-off such copy as self-protection.

This is relevant not only in terms of copy that may be contentious but to other material such as that which must comply with certain regulation such financial regulation. Whether they should get that extra protection by getting a written legal indemnity from certain clients or taking out expensive libel insurance themselves may seem extreme. However, a read through what follows will provide some guidance in deciding whether either or both options should be taken. As such, we are addressing the general question of risk management, to reduce, and hopefully eliminate, exposure to the risk of practitioners and their firms being sued for their part in publishing libellous material or, if not that, then of publishing a malicious falsehood, both causes of action which will now be discussed in a general way.

Libel

This material is not been written for students of law; nor for lawyers. Its audience are professionals working in the field of communications, albeit within certain defined limits. Therefore, the complex language of the law of defamation to which libel belongs will be kept as consumer-friendly as possible, so that readers do not get tied up in knots trying to understand technical legal language more appropriate to the courtroom or lecture theatre.

Defamation is an area of law that is called "tort." A tort is a civil wrong. We saw this when we addressed the law of negligence, which, itself, is a tort. So also is malicious falsehood, which is explained below.

Defamation is committed by the wrongful *publication* of a false or untrue statement about a *living* person, which *tends* to lower that person in the eyes of right-thinking members of society or *tends* to hold that person up to *hatred, ridicule* or *contempt*, or causes that person to be shunned or avoided by *right-thinking* members of society. A shorter, but no less effective definition of defamation is: the publication of an untrue imputation against the *reputation* of another.

Libel is the publication of defamatory matter in permanent form such as articles, caricatures and photographs published in books, newspapers and magazines, and also material broadcast on radio and television, even though these are considered transitory. Certain words have been highlighted, which will be explained:

- **Publication**: There must be publication of the untrue statement to a third party. This will be further explained shortly.
- **Living**: Unless and until the law is changed, it is not possible to libel a dead person. The law does not allow the living relatives of the deceased to sue for defamation on behalf of the deceased, to vindicate his or her reputation.
- **Tends**: The law does not say that the publication of a defamatory press release, for example, must have damaged the reputation of some person or other legal entity. The publication need only tend to injure the reputation.
- **Hatred, ridicule, contempt**: While "hatred" and "contempt" are self-explanatory, the inclusion of "ridicule" may surprise readers. A libel action over a light-hearted item in an Irish daily newspaper diary column which ridiculed a politician over allegedly paying above its value for a painting at an exhibition in the home of his party leader in order to ingratiate himself to his leader, cost the paper a substantial amount of money in a High Court jury award of damages and legal costs of the action and subsequent appeal to the Supreme Court.
- **Right-thinking**: This somewhat archaic term is meant to describe the ordinary person in the street - the reasonable person. A jury of 12 lay people is therefore considered to be composed of reasonable people who bring their common sense and judgment to bear in deciding whether what is contained in the notional press release is, in fact, defamatory or not. The judge will have already decided whether what was published is *capable* of being defamatory.
- **Reputation**: This is the most important word of all. The reason for this is that defamation is all about reputation, arguably a person's most valuable asset. And not just that of a living person but also the reputation of companies,

banks and others with legal entities. Everybody is entitled to their reputation, to their good name. It is a question of degree. It even applies to a person sent to prison for committing a crime. Again, there is a recent precedent for this in another Irish case taken successfully against a national daily by a man convicted and sentenced to three years in prison for a very serious assault on a Garda. While the man was in prison a newspaper carried a feature. It included a photograph of the prisoner and an article headed: "Isolation of Jail C Wing," in which it was stated that prisoners in this section of the prison were sexual offenders, a collection of rapists and child molesters. It stated that the section also housed other prisoners who were held there for their own protection. At the time this man was housed in "C" wing. He sued the newspaper, claiming that the words meant he was a sex offender, a child molester or rapist and was incarcerated there for his own protection. He got £60,000 damages from the jury. The paper appealed but the Supreme Court, upholding the jury finding, said the man had a "somewhat flawed reputation, but it was still a fairly serious libel." If an article is published which damages it, or tends to damage a person's reputation, then they are entitled to compensation as a consequence. That compensation is usually a sum of money, called damages.

Naming people

The parties responsible for publication of defamatory material are many. In the context in which this chapter is written it can mean any party who had anything to do with bringing the matter complained of before the public. It can mean the PR firm who wrote the material that gave rise to the action. It can also mean the client of that firm who supplied the material with which the press release was composed.

The press release was, after all, a public statement on

behalf of a company, an individual, an organisation or a group. Another party could be the journalist in the editorial department of the particular media outlet who rewrote the press release, and possibly was responsible for the libel by misspelling a name for example or by writing "not" instead of "now' in the copy. Then there is the sub-editor who edited the copy and put up a headline that could, itself, be libellous.

Being the person ultimately responsible for what appears in a newspaper or magazine, the editor is also at risk of being named as a defendant, as he or she let the libellous copy inadvertently slip through the net. Even though several parties are potentially liable, the entity that publishes the material to the world at large, the owners of the publishing company, may be the only ones whose name appears on the High Court plenary summons or Circuit Court civil bill. There is one very good reason for this – money. The proceedings will be issued against the party with the "broadest back," who can best meet the claim financially, with or without the support of an insurance policy providing an indemnity against a libel claim.

The question then arises: can a publisher be successfully sued for libel by a person not named in the offending article? The answer is an emphatic "Yes." This has happened many times. In at least three Irish cases that readily come to mind where money was paid out by newspapers – one a settlement, the other a jury award and the third a Supreme Court ruling – the three people who brought the libel actions were not named. In one case, the journalist said the individual was not even in his contemplation when he wrote the piece.

Once an individual can prove that they were identifiable or capable of being identified, then they will succeed in discharging this important proof. They do this by tendering evidence to the court. In such a case, an individual called his wife to the witnesses box to testify that after the article was published she had received 'phone calls from people who said they understood the article referred to her husband. Their children were also called to the stand to give evidence of the fact that other children had derided them in school about their father's name being in the paper.

ESSENTIALS

People who bring libel actions are obliged to prove the various aspects of the case on the balance of probabilities. Hence, on this standard of proof they were able to satisfy the court that was written referred to them.

In summary, a person taking a libel action has a number of strict proofs to discharge. These have been covered in a general way already. They are:

- The person taking the action must be able to prove to the court that he or she was the person referred to in the published copy.
- The material must be published to a third party. A press release containing a defamatory imputation about an individual or other entity will become published in this legal sense when it is read by a party other than the one mentioned in the copy.
- Of course, it is also published when it appears in a newspaper or is broadcast on radio or TV. Once the damaging material gets to the notice of a third party, publication takes place.
- The offending words must be defamatory or capable of being defamatory.

INNUENDO

Words can have different meanings: firstly, there is the plain or natural meaning or the everyday meaning of words and secondly, there is the innuendo.

It is possible to libel somebody by innuendo. As a result of a secondary or hidden meaning being brought to the words published, a totally different meaning than that intended by the author is given to the article. This state of affairs is usually brought about quite innocently.

An example of this was the action taken by a snooker hall owner in Dublin over a published comment by a reporter in a daily newspaper that "the table told lies" because a celebrated snooker player had not scored a century break while giving a snooker exhibition in the hall. The hall owner pleaded that the words meant the table was not even (flat) and he therefore was incompetent in setting up the table for the exhibition. The Supreme Court ruled that the words were defamatory or capable of being defamatory.

It can also be brought about in a situation where a newspaper reports that an individual was seen entering an address with the number of the premises given, such as no. 999 Moon Street, believed to be a grocery shop. However, unknown to the journalist and the newspaper, No. 999 Moon Street is, in fact, a brothel. Therefore, the statement is capable of having a defamatory meaning.

Intention

This might all be unfair to the innocent journalist and publisher who had no intention to write something defamatory of an individual. Journalists, authors, PR practitioners, publishers and others do not set out to deliberately defame somebody.

Far from it. But it happens, through inadvertence, mistake, carelessness or, as we have just shown, by innuendo. This brings home the very important point that 'intention' does not come into it. It does not matter what the writer or the publisher intended. What matters is whether a reasonable person reading the article thinks less of the individual concerned. Intention, as such, is irrelevant.

Danger signs

It is not possible to legislate for every eventuality. Libel can arise in a multitude of different circumstances. However, there are a couple of guidelines which practitioners should become familiar with in order to help reduce or eliminate the risk. Extreme caution should be exercised when writing copy which in any way:

- Reflects adversely on any person in their office, profession, calling, trade or business. To imply or suggest that an individual is unfit or incompetent in any of these situations is capable of being defamatory.
- Imputes that a person has committed a criminal offence. This might appear something way outside the sphere of public relations and corporate communications generally but it is not. For example, to raise a question in what might otherwise appear to be an innocent statement that somebody is "under suspicion" or of being "less than honest" would fit into this category. The word "Suspects" over the pictures and names of three politicians cost a national daily newspaper the bones of £100,000 in damages and costs in settlements.

Generally, any words that reflect adversely on a person's moral, intellectual or professional character may be defamatory and may give grounds for an action to be taken against the parties involved in the publication. These can include the newspaper or other medium, the journalist, the editor.

If it transpires that libellous copy was provided by a PR firm, for example, it is unlikely that they would be sued or joined as co-defendants with the media defendants. However, in a situation like that where libel damages are awarded, publishers, in trying to limit their financial liability for what, in reality, was somebody else's error, are entitled to seek a contribution from that party towards their financial bill, in the same way that some publishers seek a similar contribution from freelance journalists. This might seem far-fetched to the cynical but there is precedence for it.

Purchasing expensive libel insurance is hardly an option, but exercising extreme care when dealing with copy that could be regarded as contentious is.

Truth

This chapter is written specifically for those it is aimed towards. It does not dwell on the many other facets of defamation law that publishers generally need to be very familiar with, including the several defences that are available to publishers, including the proposed new one of "*reasonable publication.*" The reason for this is that PR firms and others the book is written for are not publishers in the strict sense and therefore do not require detailed technical knowledge of the law of defamation. Nevertheless, there is one very important defence that everybody should know about. That is the defence known as "justification". It is also known as the defence of "truth". And for very good reason.

If a party publishes factual material that is defamatory or capable of being defamatory, the best defence for the publisher to take if sued by the person allegedly defamed is to prove that the material was substantially true. Truth is an absolute defence.

Until the law is reformed, the defence that would be raised where the libel action arose out of published material consisting of an opinion or comment is known as 'fair comment,' that is, the publisher must prove that the comment was fair in the sense that it was the honest belief of the writer; that it was based on facts that were true and thirdly, that the comment was on a matter of public interest or benefit. The latter factor is very important in defamation law generally. This defence might also be called "honest opinion."

Reasonable publication as a defence in its own right, as set out in the Defamation Bill, is new to this country. This could be relied on by a publisher in circumstances where libellous matter was published but the publication was made in the course of, or for the purposes of, the discussion of some subject of public interest the public discussion of which was for the public benefit. Therefore, it would be argued by the publisher that it was reasonable in all the circumstances to publish the matter complained of.

It would be important to prove that there was no malice behind the particular publication. Actual malice could be described as knowledge of falsity or reckless disregard of the truth or falsity of a statement.

This was very much at the kernel of the famous *Sullivan v. New York Times* case in the United States which gave publishers a minimum standard of protection by imposing on public officials, who sued for libel, the burden of proving fault. The standard of fault required is actual malice. This *Sullivan* defence, which was later extended to public figures (people who had "assumed a role of special prominence in society") is very much a bonus for journalists writing about persons involved in public affairs. It enables them to escape liability unless the public figures and public officials can prove actual malice. As yet this defence is not available in this country.

Privilege

Malice is not only an important element in that context, it is also crucial in situations where a publisher is arguing that it had a duty to report something and that others had an interest in reading it in the particular media outlet or hearing or seeing it on radio to TV. This would be known as an occasion of qualified privilege. Examples would be public meetings to discuss matters of public interest, the reporting of tribunals or other legislative inquiries, company AGMs and local authority meetings. Certain press conferences may soon be included. That would be especially welcome for PR firms. However, the law in granting this form of privilege also imposes a caveat – the reports must be fair and accurate and not be actuated by malice. Malice destroys qualified privilege.

"Fair and accurate" are essential ingredients to get this benefit. One newspaper which reported a Question Time debate in Dail Éireann some years ago was directed by a judge to pay libel damages to a person defamed in the reporting of the debate. The judge said a combination of the headline and the introductory paragraph misrepresented what had taken place. As a result, it was not a fair or accurate report.

The media is protected by qualified privilege in certain situations under the existing legislation as contained in the Defamation Act 1961. Section 18 protects the reporting of court proceedings provided the reports are fair, accurate, are published contemporaneously (next publication or issue) and that the hearing was held in open court.

In summary

As can be seen from all of this, defamation or libel law is complex and a trap for the unwary. No effort should be spare to ensure accuracy in copy presented for publication and, if necessary, have the client sign off copy considered contentious. However, even taking these precautions, including getting specific legal advice, the vagaries of the

English language and the complexities of this law does not guarantee immunity from getting it wrong.

Malicious or injurious falsehood

While defamation or libel involves damage or injury to reputation, malicious falsehood does not. It could also be termed "slander of goods" or "slander of title." Persons who sue publishers for defamation sometimes bring a claim against the same media defendant under the head of malicious falsehood. Like defamation it is a tort or civil wrong. It involves the publication of a false statement calculated to injure a person in his trade. It is about damaging falsehoods that deceive people about an individual and his business that results in that individual suffering a loss, usually a monetary loss.

Such a falsehood would be to publish a statement or an advertisement stating that a named PR firm had gone out of business. This statement is false, it deceives the public and it causes loss to the firm because potential clients go elsewhere with their business. A party bringing a claim under this head has to prove that the falsehood was published with malice and referred to that party or to his or her property, or to an office, profession, calling, trade or business held or carried on by the individual at the time the matter was published.

Defamation Bill 2006

The long-awaited draft legislation to repeal the Defamation Act 1961 was published on July 4, 2006 and is reproduced in full later in this book (see Appendix 7). Much of it is of a technical nature and not suitable for a publication such as this which is to generally inform practitioners and students of particular laws and their effect on their practice. However, the Bill proposes to do away with the Libel and Slander – two different forms of defamation - and to replace them with one tort (a civil wrong) of defamation. A party bringing a defamation claim must do so within one year of the cause of action arising, or up to two years if a court consents. This contrasts with the present law which allows a party six years in which to commence a claim for libel and three years for a slander action.

Of the many major reforms included in the Bill is one which obliges claimants to verify in a sworn statement (affidavit) the assertions and allegations they set out in their grounding court documents, such as a High Court plenary summons and statement of claim, and a Circuit Court civil bill. A person who makes a false or misleading statement in any material respect will be prosecuted for a criminal offence. This provision should considerably help reduce the number of frivolous or vexatious, nuisance or bluff claims taken against media defendants. A claim brought in the Circuit Court will have a cap of €50,000 of the damages awarded. Juries are being retained for High Court defamation actions only.

As discussed (above) the defence of justification is to be renamed the defence of *Truth* while the defence of fair comment will become the defence of *Honest Opinion* when the Bill becomes law. The publication of an *apology* by the media to aggrieved persons will no longer involve the media in a catch 22 situation – where they were unable to contest liability or fault if they published an apology. As forecast, the Bill also introduces a new defence into Irish law of *fair and reasonable publication on a matter of public importance.* This is designed to facilitate public discussion where there is both a benefit and an interest in such discussions taking place. A range of matters are specified in section 24 of the Bill which a court must take into account in deciding whether or not the publication of a statement was fair and reasonable in the circumstances. Malice or other improper motive proved against a defendant will result in loss of this defence.

The Bill provides that defendants can lodge money in court without having to admit their liability. In other words, they will still be able to challenge every aspect of the claim taken against them. Other forms of relief for parties affected by the publication of defamatory material will also be available, including an order declaring that a published statement was false and defamatory, an order directing a defendant to publish a correction order and damages in respect of which judges will be empowered to give directions to juries in High Court defamation actions. This has been a controversial issue for many years as judges were reluctant to direct juries as to the category of awards they should make in specific cases. In future also, the Supreme Court may substitute its own award for that awarded in the High Court. This will considerably ably reduce the need for ordering expensive re-trials where the Supreme Court rules in an appeal that an award of damages by a High Court jury was excessive, for example.

The draft legislation, which facilitates the setting up of the country's first Press Ombudsman and Press Council by the Minister for Justice making an order declaring that they be "recognised" for the purposes of the Act, extends the areas to which absolute and qualified privilege applies, including to determinations and reports of the Press Ombudsman and Press Council and to certain press conferences. As with the 1961 Act all reports to which the privilege attaches must be fair and accurate. Schedule 2 of the Bill sets out the minimum requirements in relation to the Press Council.

Finally, as regards malicious falsehood (referred to above), the Bill clarifies both the basis of this tort (civil wrong) and the circumstances where special damage is, or is not, required to be shown to the court.

Chapter 10

Alternative Dispute Resolution: Arbitration

For many reasons that will become apparent arbitration is very much the preferred alternative to litigation for the settlement of disputes and it may take place when both parties agree to it.

Many contracts have a clause built into them providing that any dispute arising on the contract should be decided by arbitration. It even applies in a simple contract for the provision of a package holiday between a customer and tour operator. As with being familiar in a general way with the legal system and the courts, an insight into the law of arbitration may prove useful for practitioners, among themselves, and in their business dealings with clients.

There is a system in place to decide claims worth millions of Euro while, at the other end of the scale, there is a scheme especially set up to deal with claims of €7,500 or less.

Going back to first principles, we know that legislation and the common law confers rights which may arise under contract and in order to enforce those rights the courts were established.

In earlier chapters we have seen the multiplicity of courts in Ireland each of which has its own set of statutory rules governing its practice and procedure.

Lawyers are engaged to represent the opposing parties – always a solicitor; usually a solicitor and barrister and sometimes a solicitor, a barrister and one or two senior counsel. The higher the court, the more lawyers will represent the parties.

In addition, there are other fees, including stamp duty and VAT on the professional fees which goes to the Exchequer and helps pay the salaries of the officials who administer the courts. It is an expensive process all round added to which are two other negative aspects: slow and cumbersome. That is not to say that submitting a dispute to arbitration is cheap. The fees of the person who will adjudicate between the parties – the arbitrator – have to be paid and they could be substantial, in addition to which the parties will probably be represented by lawyers.

There is always the possibility that the dispute will end up in the High Court after arbitration but this does not happen very often. When it does, it is usually a very big case with important points of law involved and, perhaps, lots of money at stake.

Arbitration Rules

The rules which govern arbitration are laid down in legislation. In Ireland, the legislation is provided by the Arbitration Acts 1954 – 1998 and, just as the Defamation Act, 1961 failed to provide a definition of "defamation" so also did the 1954 Act omit a definition for "arbitration." However, a handy definition of arbitration is the following:

> "The submission of a disputed matter for decision to private, unofficial persons, selected in a manner provided by law or agreement."

Another way of describing it is to say that while the courts are available to people to enforce their legal rights, it is frequently open to them, if they so wish, to agree with one another that some dispute between them shall be settled, not by the courts, but by submitting to the decision of some private person on the matter, and each of them agrees to abide by the decision. This method of settling disputes is known as arbitration.

No Publicity

It has various advantages over the forum or method of adjudicating on disputes in court and a major one is the fact that hearings in arbitration proceedings are usually heard in private. This means that nobody, especially the media, will have access to the hearing other than the parties, their witnesses and lawyers.

The report or adjudication of the arbitrator is delivered privately to the parties involved. It is not unlike the new system operated by the Personal Injuries Assessment Board whereby a claimant has a claim administered and adjudicated by the Board away from the media gaze.

The only way an arbitration could become public knowledge would be if either or both parties decided to leak it to the media or announce it in some way that the media got to hear about it indirectly. Otherwise, it could only get into the public domain if a point of law arose in the arbitration which required a determination of the High Court.

In practice, there is a procedure whereby the High Court is asked to examine the arbitrator's award (finding) under the procedure known as judicial review. The arbitrator could be asked to state a case (in the same way as a judge of the District or Circuit Court can be, as discussed earlier) to the High Court. Were that to happen, the case, if considered of news value, would be reported.

The law does not allow the parties to a dispute to oust or push aside the power of the courts by entering into an agreement to go to arbitration in every case. In practice, however, this could happen, depending on whether the arbitration claim is properly put together. If the parties had originally agreed to settle any dispute arising between them by arbitration, and if one of them unilaterally decided to go to court to have the issue resolved by a judge, the other party to the dispute can apply to the court to stay the court proceedings until the arbitration is determined.

Arbitrations are very common in building construction disputes which are usually adjudicated upon by architects who are better trained and skilled to handle these technicalities than ordinary judges because of their every-day familiarity with construction.

However, before there can be an arbitration the parties must have completed a contract in which they mutually agree that their disputes must be settled in this way. They can do so before or after a dispute arose. The latter is often the case with building disputes which arise in the course of actual construction. When entering into such a contract, they may agree that a dispute shall be determined by a named person, although they do not have to nominate an arbitrator. Unlike a court where the parties cannot usually decide which judge will hear their case, the essence of arbitration is that the parties to it determine themselves who will adjudicate their dispute.

If the contract does not contain an arbitration clause, the parties may decide to go to arbitration when a dispute arises and then decide who should arbitrate it.

Appointing an Arbitrator

In making an appointment, it is usual for the parties to nominate several likely arbitrators or for a professional body such as the Law Society of Ireland or the Royal Institute of the Architects of Ireland or one of the specially trained arbitrators belonging to the Irish branch of the London-based but worldwide organisation, the Chartered Institute of Arbitrators, as examples, to nominate an arbitrator or to draw up a list of people from which a person can be appointed. These are approached informally and asked if they would act. By this process, an arbitrator is finally selected and appointed.

The level of the fees to be paid to the arbitrator is decided between him and the parties who appointed him in advance. They are jointly responsible for the arbitrator's fees which he becomes legally entitled to when he makes an award.

In fact, arbitrators have a lien (a legal claim) on the award for the amount of the fees owed for the particular arbitration, in addition to any out-of-pocket expenses. They are, therefore, entitled, not to give their award until these sums are discharged. In addition, the arbitrator is empowered to demand that the parties pay an interim payment towards his costs in advance of the hearing.

Binding

In order for it to be valid arbitration, the parties to the arbitration must intend that the decision of the arbitrator is binding on them. They must also intend that the their respective legal rights and obligations are determined by the decision.

The arbitrator's decision or award is therefore very important and is binding in much the same way as a decision by a court is. Hence the need that the formalities associated with an arbitration should be observed by all the parties to it.

The agreement by which parties refer their dispute to arbitration is known as a submission. This is normally in writing. The arbitrator cannot delegate his powers to any person but must hear and determine the issues in dispute himself. If, however, an issue of law arose in an arbitration, the arbitrator could engage the services of a lawyer to act as a legal assessor to assist him regarding the point of law that arose. In addition, the arbitrator is entitled to get legal assistance to help in finalising his adjudication.

Arbitrator's Duties

One of the first duties of the arbitrator is to decide the location, date and time for the hearing and to then inform the parties. When the arbitration does get underway, the arbitrator must hear the evidence tendered by either or both parties in the presence of both parties.

The rules of evidence associated with an ordinary constitutional court are observed by the arbitrator. The parties must consent if the arbitrator himself or herself intends to call a witness. The arbitrator must act fairly. They have extensive powers given to them by the legislation, including in relation to the conduct of the hearing itself.

The Award

Sometimes, the issues in dispute will be settled before or during the actual arbitration hearing. If not, and the dispute goes to a determination, the arbitrator will give a final decision in the form of an award. Occasionally, the arbitrator may make what's known as an interim award, involving part only of the dispute.

The award is in written form. It can be set aside in certain cases, such as where the arbitration is proved to be improperly conducted. An example would be where it is proved the arbitrator showed bias in favour of one of the parties to the arbitration. This would be a matter for the High Court or, on appeal, the Supreme Court to decide.

Enforcement

Should the party which looses the claim refuse to carry out the terms of the arbitrator's award in full, the other party may apply to the High Court to enforce compliance.

An arbitrator's award has the force of law of a court order. Solicitors are well used to representing clients at arbitrations – as are specialist barristers - and they should, of course, be consulted in the first instance with regard to arbitrations generally and how one should be progressed if it is considered a necessary alternative to going down the court route.

The Bar Council's Scheme

The Bar Council has introduced a small claims arbitration scheme designed to reduce the administration costs for the parties who bring their dispute for resolution. A bonus of the scheme is that it allows business to claim an amount of money up to a maximum of €7,500 which might ordinarily be written off as being too expensive to go to court for.

The rules are designed to make the arbitration fast, efficient and simple to process. Parties wishing to bring a claim should complete the Bar Council's submission form that is provided with the rules together with all the documents they want to produce in support of their claim. When that is done, the Bar Council will appoint an arbitrator chosen from a trained pool, who will immediately contact both parties to outline the timetable for the arbitration process, inform them of his fee and explain how the arbitration will be carried out.

It is possible that the arbitrator will decide the case based on the documents submitted by the parties. For this to happen, both parties must agree to it, in advance of course. In all other cases, there will be an oral hearing at which the parties are entitled to call evidence from witnesses supporting the respective sides. This should not last more than four hours.

Unless there are exceptional circumstances the arbitrator will make the award within 14 days of the hearing which, as in any arbitration, is binding on the parties. The case will remain confidential and the costs will be within the scale decided by the arbitration office of the Bar Council. These may be awarded against either side at the discretion of the arbitrator.

In effect, the scheme is an attempt by the Bar Council to address concerns of the business community that: legal language is sometimes inaccessible; that lack of case management allows the process to be slow and that litigation costs are sometimes excessive.

Chapter 11

Copyright, Photographers and Image Rights

The work of Public Relations and advertising practitioners involves a considerable amount of interaction with newspapers and commercial photographers who are hired under a simple contract to cover events as diverse as its possible to imagine.

This chapter will look at copyright generally and also at two very distinct areas for consideration: photographers and some aspects of the copyright law relating to their work and, secondly, a look at image rights, a very different legal concept which the common law does not, as yet, acknowledge or recognise in either Ireland.

Copyright law protects, among other things, original literary work, film, sound recordings, broadcasts and computer software. It does not protect ideas, facts or information.

Journalists begrudgingly accept the general legal principle that copyright does not protect their news stories, even though their skill and labour are very much involved in putting the report together. However, that is not to say that copyright does not exist in the verbatim reporting of a speech or spoken words once the journalist employs skill, labour and judgment in assembling the report. It could be argued that it does, in the same way as persistent "lifting" of news stories by one newspaper from another and re-publishing it without acknowledging or attributing the copy to its original source could be.

Nothing is designed to raise the blood pressure of a print

or photographic journalist more than to see their work plagiarised, especially if they are freelance because, if they are employees, their publisher will usually own the various copyrights that go into producing a newspaper or magazine, including the literary copyright in the words themselves, the artistic copyright in photographs and the layout copyright.

Publishers and magazines in some countries have a facility under which they grant permission by way of licence to parties requiring copies of articles and clippings, in the same way that tape recordings of items broadcast on radio and TV can be obtained for a fee from an independent agency.

Freelance journalists supplying copy, speculatively or on request, to media outlets should not be surprised if they're requested (or directed) to transfer *all* their rights in the material submitted. If they refuse, their copy or photographs may not be used and they consequently lose the income. If they agree, they can have no complaint if they find that the material which they produced "from the sweat of their brow" ends up in other publications, including the Internet.

The National Union of Journalists are naturally, against this practice as it deprives its members of the potential to earn more for their work. For this reason, the journalists are advised to demand higher once-off payments to compensate them for such "lost" income.

Definitions

The new copyright legislation in Ireland, the Copyrights and Related Rights Act 2000, provides some useful definitions:

- "**Artistic works**" means, among other things, photographs, prints and collages.
- "**Copyright** work" means a work in which copyright subsists.
- "**Photograph**" is defined by the 2000 Act as a recording

of light or any other radiation on any medium on which an image is produced, or from which an image may by any means be produced and which is not part of a film.

- "**Author**" means the person who creates a work and includes in the case of a photograph, the photographer. The person who takes a photograph is the author.
- **Copyright of a photograph shall expire** 70 years after the death of the photographer. If it is anonymous, it will expire 70 years after it was first made public lawfully.
- **Copyright is a property right**.

Copyright laws hit the headlines this year with the reporting of the claim of copyright infringement against the publisher of Dan Brown's best-selling book, *The Da Vinci Code* in the High Court, London by two of the authors of the book, *The Holy Blood and The Holy Grail*, Richard Leigh and Michael Baigent. Random House published both books. In 2005, a New York court rejected a similar claim for damages against Dan Brown. It alleged *The Da Vinci Code* plagiarised parts of the novels, *Daughters of God* and *The Da Vinci Legacy* but the judge ruled that any similarity was based on "unprotectable ideas."

Section 23 of the new Act denies first ownership of copyright to a journalist who is an employee of a newspaper, for example.

Take the case of photographer working for a newspaper whose work for his newspaper is published by that newspaper but is also sold on to another newspaper or put on the Internet without reference to the staff photographer or without any fee being paid to him.

The Act allows the "author in the course of employment by the proprietor of a newspaper or periodical" to make use of the photograph for any purpose other than making it available to newspapers or periodicals. The photographer could use the photograph taken in the course of his work for his employer for a book of photographs he was publishing.

This might seem far-fetched but an analogous situation occurred recently where a journalist, retired from a newspaper where he was staffed, wrote a book and included material he had gathered while working for the newspaper. He was therefore protected by section 23(2) of the 2000 Act. However, even that situation could work against a photographer if he or she had signed a contract with the employer stating that *all* photographs, even those taken during his or her spare time, were the property of the employer.

Automatic

Copyright arises automatically when the original work is created, that is from the time it is written down, provided it is the creator's own skill and effort and is not copied.

Ireland and the UK are signatories to the Universal Declaration of Human Rights and the 1971 Berne Convention. Article 27 of the Declaration states:

> "Everyone has the right to the protection of the moral and material interests resulting from any scientific, literary or artistic production of which he is the author."

The Berne Convention states:

> "Independently of the author's economic rights and even after the transfer of the said rights, the author shall have the right to claim ownership of the work and to object to any distortion, mutilation or other modification or, other derogatory action in relation to the said work which would be prejudicial to his honour or reputation." It goes on to state: "These rights shall not be subject to any formality."

Therefore, although it is not essential, it may be prudent to place the copyright symbol © followed by the author's name and the date it was created beside the published work. This gives the creator the right to stop others from exploiting the work without permission. If there is a violation or infringement of the copyright, an action may be taken claiming damages and possibly an injunction to stop further copyright infringements.

Fair Dealing

Fair dealing (or fair use) exceptions also apply. The author's permission is not required if a work is being used for research or private study, provided the rights of the copyright owner are not prejudiced. It allows for reporting which takes quotations from books and plays, films and broadcasts for the purpose of writing a critique, a story or feature. However, the author and the title of the work must be *acknowledged*. Making copious copies of an author's work is unlikely to qualify as fair dealing.

In order to violate or infringe a photographer's copyright, for example, a "*substantial*" part of the work must have been copied. What constitutes "*substantial*" would depend on the circumstances of each individual case. Users of library facilities in Ireland will be familiar with the copyright warning of copyright infringement related to the copying of works that have appeared on library notice boards since the enactment of the Copyright and Related Rights Act 2000.

Assignment of Owner's Right

The owner of a copyrighted photograph can assign or pass it on to somebody else. This is done by one or other of the legal process of granting a licence or an assignment, depending on the author's intention. Assigning rights means somebody else becomes the *owner*, while the term giving it under licence means another party can *use* the copyrighted photograph or material.

Such assignments and licences can apply to *all* the rights in the photograph or material or to just one or some of the rights. A good example would be where a photographer of a copyrighted photograph gave an assignment or licence to specifically reproduce the photograph in a book but the photographer retained all other rights.

Granting permission to a publisher to reproduce an author's work means giving that publisher *rights clearance* to that work. A typical clearance might read: I confirm that I have no objection to publication by XYZ Media Ltd and its affiliates of material submitted by me for inclusion in the newspaper/magazine and I hereby grant for the term of the copyright non-exclusive rights to XYZ Media Ltd, including subsidiary rights. I confirm that this grant of publishing rights extends to all material submitted by me for publication in XYZ Media Ltd.

Contract

Public relations and advertising photographic transactions are very varied, involving any number of different circumstances However, the law of contract can be very important in terms of the ownership of photographs.

Much of the case law relating to ownership of photographs originated in the courts of North America. In one such noted case in the early part of the last century, involving pictures of French boxer, Georges Carpentier, a judge decided that the usual contract between a photographer and his customer was one of employment; that the production of the photograph was work done for the customer, not for the photographer, and the sitter was entitled to all the proprietary rights in it.

> "The work is done for the person procuring it to be done, and the negative, so far as it is a picture, or capable of reproducing pictures, of that person, and all photographs, so made from it, belong to the person."

The judge decided, in effect, that the photographer was a trustee for the purchaser who had paid him for the original pictures.

However, the opposite is true when a **staff photographer** – the term employed to describe a full-time employee – takes the photographs. In this situation ownership of the photographs belongs to the photographer's employer.

This is recognised in the 2000 Act (above). If a PR company or advertising agency employed that staff photographer in his or her spare times on, what's known as, a "nixer" different considerations would apply. Does the photographer then become an independent contractor or an employee under the control of the new employer? It would be very much in the interest of both parties – the photographer and the new employer – to have a clear legal understanding of their respective positions, preferably in writing.

This may seem far-fetched in terms of the kind of relationship and arrangements that in reality would exist which could best be described as *ad hoc*. Nevertheless, such PR and advertising employers need to have a clear-cut understanding as to the rights that attach to both sides in order to prevent any future related problems.

If a photographer decides to take pictures on his or her own initiative without being financially rewarded and is not otherwise employed, it can be said that the photographs and the property in them belong to him or her and can reproduce them freely. In an almost similar situation, a photographer is invited to an event to photograph the attendance or group such as schoolroom pictures and is not paid by the person who issued the invitation, the photographer is free to charge each person who buys his photographs because the photographer owns the photographs in this situation.

In what amounts to a situation familiar to event organisers, PR and advertising personnel, a freelance photographer could be commissioned to take photographs at an event, after which the organiser selects the picture or pictures considered most appropriate to suit a purpose such as, for example, for future promotional work relating to the event or to illustrate an article in a newspaper, magazine or promotional literature.

When the photograph is selected and then purchased by the organiser or other personnel as mentioned above, it becomes their property, not the photographer's. Such a situation could give rise to problems. Take for instance where the photographer believes the pictures that were not bought by the organiser were his or hers and they then sell them privately. To avoid this happening, PR practitioners, advertising executives or other such organiser should make their instructions to the photographer perfectly clear at the outset and agree a sum of money for the commission.

This sum may have to be considerably higher than expected to take account of the full property in the photographer's work on a specific occasion, including the negatives, which most photographers consider as their own property. However, the creation of such an agreement will have the desired effect of giving them full control of all of the photographs taken on the occasion. Once the photographer agrees to the terms – in which he or she will have an input with regard to some of the terms including the price – the law implies the existence of a contract, which binds both sides.

These situations are not clear-cut, one reason why it is essential for the parties to agree terms at the outset and to reduce those terms to writing, if necessary. Intellectual property law, which incorporates copyright law, is very specialised and what is stated in this chapter is merely for general guidance.

Specific advice should be taken from a lawyer expert in this field when the need arises to protect intellectual property rights in original photographs and other copyright works in this digital age.

Penalties for breach of copyright include damages and injunctions to restrain further breaches are available to copyright holders as well as criminal prosecutions.

In a civil action, if such a party can satisfy the High Court that he believes his rights are being infringed by, for example, the pirating or unlawful copying of works such as CDs, DVDs or videos, the judge will grant what's known as an *Anton Pillar* order which allows the copyright holder to raid the venue where the copying is taking place and to seize the copying equipment and pirated goods.

Image Rights

In October, 2005, Lee Trundle, a striker contracted with League One club, Swansea, until the end of the 2005/2006 season, was reported as having negotiated a lucrative image-rights deal with his club under which he was to receive a one-off payment in recognition of the amount of money the club made from sales of merchandise relating to the footballer's image. A club spokesman said: "Most of the merchandising Swansea sell is linked to Trundle. It is a deal that is mutually beneficial to both parties."

That deal, in a nutshell, adequately describes and illustrates in simple terms what image rights are all about. The player's club acknowledged the part played by him in selling merchandise for the club's benefit. As a player Trundle proved a great success and that success rubbed off in sales of the club's merchandise, such as football shirts.

In the professional game at least, clubs are slow to acknowledge a player's image rights and the part it plays in adding to the club's coffers. This is so for one very good reason – the club buys the player who is *under contract* to play for and represent the club in a particular sport and any added benefit for the club due to the player's success as a player is part of the contract negotiated between the club and the player.

At present, the common law does not recognise the existence of image rights or appropriation of personality in Ireland or the UK?

The concept of rights in a person's image exists in the USA and Canada. In the latter, the tort or civil wrong known as appropriation of personality has been judicially recognised for more than 30 years. Unauthorised use of a person's image entitles the person to compensation in some countries.

This is allied to the tort or civil wrong known as "**passing-off**," several cases of which have been taken in the High Court in Dublin over the years. This is where a party passes off the goods or services belonging to another party as its own and without the true owner's consent. It is taking advantage of the owner's reputation or goodwill in the marketplace and the essence of it is that it confuses the buying public into thinking they are buying the original goods or services.

However, in another case, the judge said there was no danger of confusion on the part of the public but the false misrepresentation was that racing driver, Eddie Irvine had endorsed the use of his image in connection with the defendant's business. Mr Irvine, from Northern Ireland, brought a successful passing-off action arising out of the unauthorised use of his image to promote advertising on a radio station devoted exclusively to sport.

The courts may view image rights or the appropriation of personality as an extension of "**passing-off**" law. Branded merchandise and celebrity endorsements are big business, not alone in Ireland but across the globe.

High-profile cases in the English courts raise issues already mentioned in the chapter on privacy but they also raised the question of whether people's images were their own private property. In *Douglas and Catherine Zeta Jones v. Hello Ltd,* the House of Lords said:

> "Recognition of the right of a celebrity to make money out of publicising private information about himself, including his photographs on a private occasion, breaks new ground."

If a sporting figure or personality has an inherent right to prevent others from exploiting their image without permission or reward, why then should the common law not recognise or acknowledge the existence of personality rights, including one's image rights? Image rights can only be protected by the aforementioned tort of passing-off, by a claim for trademark or copyright infringement, or by laws of libel and malicious or injurious falsehood as covered in chapter 9.

The failure of the law to recognise image rights, as such, remains a matter of debate in Ireland and other countries where questions have been raised over the ownership of image rights and whether it should be the individual, the team, the league or the association that they play in.

Members of the Gaelic Players' Association have been in dispute with the GAA over their image rights while, in addition, a GAA-backed PlayStation computer football game was forced to use generic players rather than identifiable ones. The GPA had offered its cooperation if real images were used but no agreement was reached with the GAA.

Many of Ireland's leading GAA players have assigned their image rights to the GPA which then owns the image rights and, consequently, represents them in negotiations with corporate and other sponsors to the financial benefit of the individual players. In this way, the players' image rights are protected from exploitation by the GPA, which engages specialist intellectual property lawyers to legally represent the players.

So, while the law does not, as yet, recognise image rights,

many big corporations and sporting organisations do. There is lots of money at stake but much of the confusion and attitude taken up by opposing parties could be overcome by looking at what players like Lee Trundle and clubs and organisations like Swansea have achieved, by recognising the worth and value of each other to each other above and beyond normal contractual relations.

The blurring of the law with regard to image rights is causing difficulty for a range of interests that PR and advertising practitioners may identify with, including sponsors willing to enter into lucrative contracts for individuals with valuable images who can enhance sales of products and services. A written contract with the respective rights, including image rights, clearly set out and accepted as part of membership of club, organisation or association would appear to be in the best interests of all parties.

There is a provision in the new Privacy Bill, 2006 which can be interpreted as protecting image rights. It is contained in section 3(2) which identifies certain acts as violating an individual's privacy, including "*to use the name likeness or voice of the individual, without the consent of that individual*" for a number of purposes without financial gain to the person. These include for advertising or promoting the sale of, or trade in, any property or service. There are a number of things that a claimant would have to prove, principally that the person knew that that individual had not given such consent.

CHAPTER 12

Freedom of Information and Data Protection

Those of us with memory stretching back a few decades will testify to the secrecy that was innate within officialdom in Ireland. Journalists more than most had cause to decry a perceived censorship reminiscent of the troubled years when the Government Censor had to run his red pen through editorial copy before newspapers were put to bed each night. Journalists of that era despised and railed against such interference with newspaper publishing, which was abhorrent to the very notion of press freedom that was subsequently given expression as a personal right in the fundamental rights section of the 1937 Constitution. That provision in Article 40 states:

> "The State guarantees liberty for the exercise of the following rights, subject to public order and morality: The right of the citizens to express freely their convictions and opinions. The education of public opinion being, however, a matter of such grave import to the common good, the State shall endeavour to ensure that organs of public opinion, such as the radio, the press, the cinema, while preserving their rightful liberty of expression, including criticism of Government policy, shall not be used to undermine public order or morality or the authority of the State…".

Despite the existence of this guarantee by the State, journalists would argue that this fundamental right merely paid lip service to a valued aspiration because of the continued existence of the culture of secrecy within the civil service and the administration of the State generally. They were unable to extract information from Government departments and public bodies that they saw as being important in the public interest. That was to change with the enactment of legislation that came into effect on April 28, 1998, the Freedom of Information Act 1997 (hereafter referred to as FOI). It represented an extraordinary and welcome change in attitude – a seed change, if you will – that, no doubt, has benefited the media, communications generally and the public alike with the release and publishing of information that may have remained confidential to those charged with its administration and secret from those people who were, in many situations, most affected by it.

Purpose of Legislation

The head note to the Act gives a broad view of the purposes of the Act:

- to enable members of the public to obtain access, to the greatest extent possible consistent with the public interest and the right to privacy, to information in the possession of public bodies and
- to enable persons to have personal information relating to them in the possession of such bodies corrected and, accordingly, to provide for a right of access to records held by such bodies, for necessary exceptions to that right and for assistance to persons to enable them to exercise it,
- to provide for the independent review both of decisions of such bodies relating to that right and of the operation of this Act generally,

- to provide for the establishment of the office of Information Commissioner and to define its functions, to provide for the publication of such bodies of certain information about them relevant to the purposes of this Act,
- to amend the Official Secrets Act 1963, and
- to provide for related matters.

The Act, which was amended by the Freedom of Information Act 2003, apart from obliging Government departments, Health Service Executive Areas, local authorities and a broad range of other statutory bodies to provide information on their activities and to make personal information available to the public, gave three new statutory rights: to access information held by public bodies, to amend official information relating to oneself amended where it was incomplete, incorrect or misleading and to obtain reasons for decisions affecting oneself. Information about public bodies is contained in a manual that every public body is obliged to publish.

Right of Access

While the right to privacy of individuals is paramount in the Act, there is a right of access to all information, provided its disclosure does not harm the general public or invade somebody's privacy. The golden thread running through the criminal law in this country is the presumption of innocence – an accused person is presumed innocent until a court of law proves them otherwise beyond a reasonable doubt. Similarly, the FOI introduced a presumption of *openness*, which entitled an applicant to the information sought unless clear specific reasons were given for not disclosing it. These are known as exceptions. The Act distinguished between two types of official information: personal information, meaning confidential data, and official records relating to information in any form. It is this latter type that journalists, public relations, public affairs and other practitioners in the field of business and political communications would be most interested in.

This new law was viewed as a "seed change" in attitude and, according to the current Information Commissioner, represented "a transformational development" in the relationship between members of the public and the State, although citing a number of cases in her annual report where her Office had difficulty in extracting information it was entitled to under the FOI.

The Commissioner acts as an independent referee to whom applicants refused access to information by public bodies can appeal to, although an increased regular fee of €150, and €50 for others, including medical card holders, for each such appeal, may be one hurdle too many to cross in pursuit of particular information. If the Commissioner rejects an appeal, the applicant has a right to initiate a High Court action against the refusal on a point of law and, subsequently, a further appeal to the Supreme Court.

If the Commissioner lost in the High Court, she, also, has a right of appeal to the Supreme Court which, in January, 2006, rejected such an appeal by the Information Commissioner. This was a case in which a father, a widower, who had been separated from his late wife, claimed (successfully) to be entitled to under the FOI to information, in the form of hospital notes, about an illness of his daughter, albeit he first sought the information in 2000.

Should be Greater Use of FOI

Despite the availability of this valuable mechanism to extract official information, journalists and others could, perhaps, be criticised for not using the Act enough in the search for information. After all, the idea of good investigative journalism is to "look under rocks" in search of information that others do not want to reveal.

The FOI has been extended to many departments, bodies

and agencies since its inception in 1998. In fact, the Minister for Finance announced his intention to extend it to a further 109 public bodies later in 2006.

However, earlier this year, the Information Commissioner, Emily O'Reilly, a former political journalist, earlier this year said it was difficult to see why the Act had not been extended to all public bodies and emphasised that many bodies "of significance" remained outside the scope of the Act. She listed these as including An Garda Síochána, the Judicial Appointments Advisory Board, the Private Security Authority, the Central Bank, the Financial Services Authority, the Adoption Board, the Irish Red Cross, the Personal Injuries Assessment Board, the Office of the Refugee Applications Commissioner and the office of the Refugee Tribunal.

The bodies covered by the FOI include all Government departments, State agencies and bodies, county, city, borough and town councils, regional authorities, health service executive, voluntary hospitals, bodies providing services for persons with intellectual and physical disability, bodies in the broadcasting sector and in third level education, the fisheries boards.

How to Apply

In the event that the information sought is not available on request from the designated information officer in a particular public body or from the considerable amount of written material usually available from public bodies, a request in writing must be made to the FOI unit in the public body, referring, of course, to the Freedom of Information Act.

If the Act is not mentioned, the request will be dealt with as an ordinary inquiry. The standard fee for the initial request is €15 (a reduced fee of €10 for medical card holders and others). Requests should be as specific as possible so that the information can be retrieved as quickly as possible. A sample application form to request information under the FOI is available at the site of the Information Commissioner under the heading "FOI Act and Regulations." This should be completed and sent to the FOI Unit of the public body or office from which the record is being sought.

The application must be acknowledged within two weeks of the date in which the request was submitted. This acknowledgement must contain the date they received the request and the name of the person dealing with it.

The date is important because time starts then and a response must be given not later than "28 days" (*i.e.* four calendar weeks) after receipt of the initial application. Therefore, if it is a clear-cut case, the information will be furnished within four weeks. However, if the record is held by another body, the original body or office must pass the request under the FOI to the second body within two weeks. This has the effect of extending the time and means that an applicant may have to wait up to six weeks for a decision. Practitioners should also be aware that there are grounds for extending the 28-day limit, such as where the request involved a large number of records.

If a practitioner is not happy with the response from the public body to any aspect of the request for information such as a refusal, the form of access to the information or the charges, or if a response is not received within four weeks of the application being made, the Act regards this as constituting a refusal by the body or office to furnish the information. This decision can be reviewed by more senior members of staff within the public body. Such applications should be submitted to the FOI Unit of the particular body.

The charge for seeking to have the decision re-examined is €75 (the reduced charge is €25). (There is no fee for a request for personal information). This review must be made within three weeks. If the outcome remains a refusal, an appeal can then be taken to the Information Commissioner, 18 Lower Leeson Street, Dublin 2.

Data Protection

Data protection is provided for in the Data Protection Acts, 1988 and 2003. This legislation gives effect to the Convention for the Protection of Individuals with regard to the Automatic Processing of Personal Data 1981. It seeks to regulate the "*collection, processing, keeping, use and disclosure*" of certain information relating to individuals that is processed automatically.

Security and privacy of personal data are paramount to the purposes of the legislation. It applies to many individuals and organisations, who keep information regarded as sensitive about lay people on computer and who therefore should be registered under the Acts.

Individuals and organisations who feel that the legislation applies to them and who wish to register should apply for information to the Data Protection Commissioner, Block 4, Irish Life Centre, Talbot Street, Dublin 1. Forms can be obtained from the office or, alternatively, can be downloaded from the Commissioner's website: www.dataprivacy.ie. There is a small fee for registration which is renewable annually.

Definitions

Some definitions are necessary to give an understanding of the legislation: Data means information that can be processed; Processing data means disclosing data; Personal data is data relating to a *living* individual who can be identified either from the data or from the data in conjunction with other information in the possession of the data controller; Data controller is a person who, either alone or with others, controls the contents and use of personal data.

In England, the original Data Protection Act 1984 was replaced by the Data Protection Act 1998. The Irish and English legislation only applies to persons who are living.

Of course, when a person dies, many of their rights die with them, including the right to privacy which, as we have seen earlier, is not generally recognised by the common law.

Data Protection Commissioner

The Data Protection Commissioner has legal powers to ensure that people's rights under the legislation are upheld, e.g. if a person having control of personal information refuses a request for access or refuses to correct inaccurate information.

Equally, if a person suffers damage because information about them is mishandled on computer, they may be entitled to claim compensation in the courts. Just as a certain people such as solicitors, doctors, architects, engineers, bankers owe a duty of care to people relying on them in the provision of a service, the data protection legislation expressly makes clear that organisations who hold personal data owe a duty of care to the person to whom the data relates. Access to their personal information must be afforded by people and organisations storing personal information on computer to individuals seeking it and, in addition, they are obliged to correct or delete any information which is found to be inaccurate or irrelevant.

Other responsibilities given to them include obtaining personal information fairly and openly, using it in ways compatible with the purpose for which it was given initially, securing it against unauthorised access or loss and making sure the information is maintained accurately and up-to-date. Also, they cannot retain the information longer than is necessary for the purpose for which it was given. If any persons or organisations fail to observe these principles, they would be in breach of the legislation and liable to be prosecuted by the Data Protection Commissioner as a result.

The Commissioner's website contains details of a complaint investigated by his office which sends out warning signals to every employer. The complaint was from a person who had applied for a specialised medical post with a major hospital. When applying for the post he had forwarded his CV together with a letter stating that he withheld consent to the hospital contacting the referees listed in his CV until "mutual interest" had been established and he had time to appraise the referees of his intentions. He was subsequently contacted by the human resources section informing him that they had already contacted the referees. When the Data Protection Commissioner took the matter up with the hospital authorities, they immediately acknowledged the error that the person's wishes had been overlooked by contacting the referees.

The Commissioner found that contacting the referees without consent was in contravention of section 2 (1)(c)(ii) of the 1998 Act. This states, in part, that data shall not be further processed in a manner incompatible with that purpose or those purposes. "Processing" was defined by the Acts as including disclosing data. He said: "A fundamental principle of the Data Protection Acts is that personal data should not be disclosed to third parties without the data subject's consent or unless one of the exemptions provided for in section 8 of the Act applied."

Unsolicited Communications or "Cold Calling'

In November 2003, the Taoiseach, Mr. Ahern signed into law Regulation 13 of Statutory Instrument 535, or to give it its full title, the European Communities (Electronic Communications Networks and Services) (Data Protection and Privacy) Regulations, 2003. This has particular significance for people working in public relations, marketing and advertising because, under it, the sending of unsolicited electronic communications from within the Republic of Ireland for the purpose of direct marketing is, in certain situations, an offence. Similar secondary legislation operates throughout the EU.

An e-mail, SMS, MMS or a fax for the purpose of direct marketing cannot be sent to an individual unless that person has given prior consent to receiving it. The same applies with regard to direct marketing telephone calls to an individual's phone number if the recipient has previously told the caller they do not want to receive such calls, or if the individual has his or her preference not to receive marketing calls noted in the National Directory Database. This is a list of all telephone numbers contained in public phone books or available through directory inquiries. Where the recipient is not an individual – a business number or e-mail address, including those associated with individuals in a business con text – a phone call may be made or an SMS/MMS/e-mail or fax sent for the purpose of direct marketing, as long as the sender has respected any opt-out preference expressed by the recipient.

Enforcement of this law is the responsibility of the Data Protection Commissioner to whom complaints can be made in writing by persons who believed they had received commercial communications in contravention of the legislation.

Case History

Where a person is successfully prosecuted, a fine of up to a maximum of €3,000 per message sent can be imposed by the court. The first prosecution under this law resulted in a fine of €300 per count in five counts being imposed by the District Court against a company convicted of sending marketing messages to five mobile phones without the consent of the recipients. The company was also ordered to pay €1,000 in costs. After the case, the Commissioner, Mr. John Meade, said the case sent a positive signal to the marketing community and to those that were targets of its promotions.

Chapter 13

Advertising, Equality, Bullying and Harassment

Advertising Standards

An advertisement is defined as a paid-for commercial communication addressed to the public or a section of it, the purpose being to influence the behaviour of those to whom it is addressed. It is characteristic of an advertisement that an advertiser pays or rewards a third party for communicating a message. Practitioners in public relations and corporate communications generally interact with advertising requirements in various ways, although with regard to public relations, the code itself does not apply to press releases and other public relations material. Generally, certain standards must be maintained as set out in Codes enforced by the Advertising Standards Authority of Ireland (ASAI).

There is a substantial amount of domestic and EU law governing advertising across a very wide range of professions, organisations and interests, such as for example the Solicitors (Advertising) Regulations 1996, the Medicinal Preparations (Advertising) Regulations 1993–1996, the European Communities (Cosmetic Products) Regulations 1997–2000, Tobacco Products (Control of Advertising, Sponsorship and Sales Promotion) Regulations 1991–2000, not to mention a host of Acts, ranging from the Consumer Information Act 1978 to the Broadcasting Act 2001. However, the ASAI has no role to play in enforcing legislation.

The Authority invites complaints regarding advertisements from the public and then resolves those complaints. It does not act as an arbitrator between conflicting ideologies, nor does it deal with contractual relationships between advertisers and consumers.

The identity of people who bring complaints to the ASAI remains confidential unless a commercial or other interest is involved. Complaints must be in writing and anonymous complaints are not pursued. Misleading advertisements and advertisements that cause offence represent the main causes of complaint each year to the ASAI, a founder member of the Brussels-based European Advertisement Standards Alliance set up in 1992 to promote and strengthen advertisement self-regulation in Europe.

There are specific codes with respect to the advertising of health and beauty, slimming, advertising and children, alcoholic drinks, financial services and products, distance selling (mail order and direct response), employment and business opportunities, occasional trading and environmental claims.

Application of Code

Generally, the Code of Advertising Standards applies to:

(a) advertisements in newspapers, magazines and other printed publications, including free sheets,

(b) posters and other promotional media in public places,

(c) brochures, leaflets, circulars, mailings and fax transmissions,

(d) commercial broadcast or television or radio or screened in cinemas,

(e) advertisements carried on audiotapes, videotapes, view data services, the Internet and all other electronic and computer systems,

(f) sales promotion material, and

(g) advertisement features and promotions.

The Code does *not* apply to:

(a) statutory, public, garda and other official notices,

(b) material published as a matter of record only,

(c) fly posting,

(d) packages, wrappers, labels and tickets unless they advertise another product or a sales promotion or are recognisable in an advertisement,

(e) point-of-sale displays, except those covered by the Code of Sales Promotion Practice or when part of a wider advertising campaign,

(f) advertisements whose principal purpose is to express the advertiser's position on a political, religious, industrial relations, social or aesthetic matter or on an issue of public interest or concern, and

(g) classified private advertisements.

Neither does the Code apply to the contents of books and editorial material in the media, nor to private correspondence, oral communication, including telephone calls, and works of art. Specialised advertisements addressed to the medical and allied professionals are outside the pervue of the code as are advertising for premium rate telephone calls and advertisements in foreign media.

Each case is considered on its own merits by the ASAI when applying the Code and the fact that it invites comment on a complaint does not mean it accepts the complainant's view. Conformity with the Code is assessed in the light of "an advertisement's probable effect when taken as a whole and in context."

The Authority pays particular attention to the characteristics of the likely audience, the media by means of which the advertisement is communicated, the location and context of the advertisement, the nature of the advertised product and the nature, content and form of any **associated** material made available or action recommended by consumers.

The ASAI works in conjunction with the main advertising organisations in Ireland: the *Association of Advertisers in Ireland* and the *Institute of Advertising Practitioners*. They do this to ensure that people employed in the relevant agencies and the media are aware of the ASAI and its codes. Apart from resolving consumer complaints, the Authority provides a further service, giving advice to the industry regarding advertising copy. Advertisers, agencies and the media can get advice on whether a proposed advertisement or sales promotion conforms with code requirements.

Rules

The general rules of the ASAI, containing the principle that all advertisements should be *legal, decent, honest and truthful,* are reproduced in Appendix 4 at page 143 by kind permission of the Authority.

Codes under Review

The ASAI codes are currently under review as is the General Advertising Code of the Broadcasting Commission of Ireland (BCI). It is developing a code that will apply to all radio and television broadcasters licensed in the State. The new code will address principles and rules that apply to all **advertising** broadcast by licensed operators. It is provided for in section 19 of the Broadcasting Act 2001. The existing framework for statutory regulation of general advertising has been in place for 11 years. Considerable change has taken place in the interim, both to advertising and sponsorship techniques as well as in the range of products and services now available to the consumer.

The BCI are keen to see the development of a code "which reflects the Commission's own regulatory principles and which enshrines the principles of protecting the citizen and the consumer," said Mr Conor Maguire SC, chairperson of the BCI.

Other Topics

There are many and varied pieces of legislation governing the employment of persons in all types of employment in Ireland, not least in public relations, advertising and others in the field of communication. Equality is high among these.

Equality

Legislation makes unlawful discrimination in employment, vocational training, **advertising**, collective agreements, the provisions of goods and services and other opportunities to which the public have access. This is contained in the Employment Equality Acts 1998 and 2004 and the Equal Status Acts 2000-2004. There are nine individual grounds on which a claim of discrimination can be taken against an employer:

- Gender: a man, a woman or a transsexual. (Specific protection is provided for pregnant employees or in relation to maternity leave).
- Marital status: single, married, separated, divorced or widowed.

- Family status: a parent of a person aged under 18 years or the resident primary carer or a parent of a person with a disability.
- Age: this applies to all ages above the maximum age at which a person is statutorily obliged to attend school.
- Disability: includes people with physical, intellectual, learning, cognitive or emotional disabilities and a range of medical conditions.
- Race: a particular race, skin colour, nationality or ethnic origin.
- Sexual orientation: gay, lesbian, bisexual or heterosexual.
- Religious belief: different religious belief, background, outlook or none at all.
- Membership of the Traveller community: people commonly called Travellers, who are identified both by Travellers and others as people with a shard history, culture and traditions, identified historically as a nomadic way of life on the island of Ireland.

Discrimination is defined as the treatment of a person in a less favourable way than another person is, has been or would be treated on any of the nine grounds. It has specific meaning under the Acts. This includes: direct discrimination, indirect discrimination, discrimination by imputation and discrimination by association.

Direct discrimination is the treatment of a person in a less favourable way than another person is, has been or would be treated in a comparable situation on any of the nine grounds which exists, existed, may exist in the future, or is imputed to the person concerned. The instruction to discriminate is prohibited also. Indirect discrimination occurs where there is less favourable treatment in effect or by impact.

Discrimination by association occurs where a person

associated with another person is treated less favourably because of that association.

Discriminatory Advertising

The legislation prohibits the classification of jobs by reference to sex and also prohibits **advertising** that discriminates on the basis of sex. Therefore, an advertisement which invites applications from one sex only is discriminatory.

Where an advertisement refers to the job in terms which imply that it is only open to a particular sex, e.g. foreman or barman, the advertisement must expressly state that the job is open to men and women.

It is unlawful for an employer to discriminate directly or indirectly on grounds of sex or marital status in recruitment, conditions of employment, and in training and promotion. This is illustrated by a case decided in the early 1980s which arose out of a brief job interview during which the applicant's marital status was the only matter discussed. The Employment Appeals Tribunal ruled the applicant had been discriminated against even though the discrimination did not affect the outcome.

Bullying and Harassment

Bullying and harassment in the workplace, a developing jurisprudence in Irish law, is unlawful under the Employment Equality Acts that, as explained (above), outlaws discrimination on nine distinct grounds. There are a number of remedies available to employees, principally under health and safety legislation and breach of contract.

Employers should have a policy on preventing and dealing with bullying and harassment. Workers should also have an input. Just as there is an implied covenant in every tenancy agreement that the tenant is entitled to peaceful enjoyment of the premises, so also is there an implied term in every contract of employment that employees have a right to a workplace free from bullying, threats, harassment and intimidation.

Definitions

The accepted definition of "bullying" is:

> "Repeated, inappropriate behaviour, direct or indirect, whether verbal, physical or otherwise, conducted by one or more persons against another or others, at the place of work or in the course of employment, which could reasonably be regarded as undermining the individual's right to dignity at work. An isolated incident of behaviour described in this definition may be an affront to dignity at work but, as a once-off incident, is not considered to be bullying."

This definition is taken from the Health and Safety Authority's 2001 (HSA) report of the Taskforce on the Prevention of Workplace Bullying entitled *Dignity at Work: The Challenge of Workplace Bullying*. It can also be described as repeated and systematic aggression, verbal, psychological or physical, conducted by an individual or group against another person or persons which may involve vindictive, cruel, malicious or humiliating at attempts to undermine a person or a group of people. It could also include giving repeated impossible deadlines or impossible tasks, imply threats, attacking a worker's reputation by rumour, gossip, innuendo or ridicule.

Some of this bullying behaviour could, conceivably, form the basis of a civil action for damages for defamation that could be brought by the employee against the employer who is vicariously liable for the civil wrongs of its servants or agents, *i.e.* its employees, no matter at what level of management they are. Examples of bullying behaviour include personal insults, persistent unjustified criticism or sarcasm, public or private humiliation or name-calling. What constitutes "bullying" depends on the particular circumstances of each individual case.

Harassment, which is governed by the Employment Equality Act, 1998, can be described as any act or conduct that is unwelcome and offensive, humiliating or intimidating on a discriminatory ground including words or gestures. It could also include the production, display or circulation of written material or pictures.

Sexual harassment includes *unwelcome* and *offensive*, *humiliating* or *intimidating* actions of a sexual nature that involves acts of physical intimacy, spoken words, gestures or the production, display or circulation of written material or pictures, or requests for sexual favours.

Stated shortly, harassment is a specific form of discrimination in relation to a person's condition of employment. As such it is based on one or more of the nine grounds referred to above on which a claim for discrimination can be taken against an employer.

The law takes a very serious view of harassment in all its forms. It can be a **criminal** offence under the Non-Fatal Offences Against the Person Act 1997 which specifically created this new offence. Section 10 of the Act states that any person who, without lawful authority or reasonable excuse, by any means including by use of the telephone, harasses another by persistently following, watching, pestering, besetting or communicating with him or her, shall be guilty of an offence.

The legislation defines harassment by one person against another as occurring where (a) he or she, by his or her acts intentionally or recklessly, seriously interferes with the other's peace and privacy or causes alarm, and (b) his or her acts are such that a reasonable person would realise that the acts would seriously interfere with the other's peace and privacy or cause alarm, distress or harm to the other. A person found guilty by the District Court of harassment is liable to be fined up to a maximum of €1500 or to imprisonment for 12 months, or both. A fine or a prison term of up to 7 years or both could be imposed if convicted on indictment by the Circuit Court.

Anti-bullying Policy

The HSA's Code of Practice on the Prevention of Workplace Bullying makes it imperative on all employers to put in place a safety consultation programme that facilitated participation by all employees in health and safety matters. This would include an anti-bullying policy which would facilitate the training of persons to deal with, among other relevant issues, bullying complaints.

One organisation has put in place the following formal procedure to deal with complaints, which could serve as a template for others to follow:

- The personnel officer or human resources manager forms an investigation team to carry out a thorough investigation of the complaint. The team members have already received appropriate training.
- The investigation is carried out in accordance with the principles of natural justice that ensures that each party has the right to present their side of the story and to be represented by an appropriate person of their choice.
- When the team has concluded its investigation, they will prepare a report for the personnel officer or human resources manager who, in turn, notifies to the recipient, the alleged harasser and the organisation heads.
- If a complaint is upheld, a disciplinary hearing takes place in accordance with the organisation's disciplinary procedures.

The recipients of such behaviour in the normal course of events have a number of avenues open to them to bring claims. Where the employee had no option but to resign, with or without notice, as a result of bullying, they can mount a claim for unfair **or** wrongful dismissal. In the latter instance, they would sue on foot of their contract of employment and its implied term. This would be a claim at common law for damages for breach of contract which would normally be heard by the High Court. Such claimants are usually taken by senior staff and management.

If the claim for unfair dismissal is taken under the Unfair Dismissals Acts 1977–1993 for breach of the legislation, it would be taken before a Rights Commissioner or in the Employment Appeals Tribunal. Apart from suing for unfair dismissal, they can also bring a claim for damages for personal injuries, particulars of the claim being that their health had suffered as a result of the bullying or harassment. This would be enhanced by the built-in claim for special damages made up of, among other things, loss of wages which could make the claim a very substantial one. It is incumbent on employees with a grievance to notify senior management of it in the first instance.

APPENDIX 1

European Code of Professional Conduct in Public Relations (Code of Lisbon)

Officially adopted at the General Assembly of CERP in Lisbon, April 16, 1978, and adopted by all the 18 National Associations (from 15 European Countries) who are institutional members of CERP.

Section 1 - Criteria and standards of professional qualification of practitioners bound by this Code

Clause 1

Every professional member of (national association) duly admitted as such in accordance with the rules of (national association) is deemed for the purpose of this Code to be a public relations practitioner, and to be bound by the Code.

Section 2 - General professional obligations

Clause 2

In the practice of his profession the pr practitioner undertakes to respect the principles set forth in the Universal Declaration of Human Rights, and in particular the freedom of expression and the freedom of the press which give effect to the right of the individual to receive information, within the limits of professional confidence. He likewise undertakes to act in accordance with the public interest and not to harm the dignity or integrity of the individual.

Clause 3

In his professional conduct, the pr practitioner must show honesty, intellectual integrity and loyalty. In particular, he undertakes not to make use of comment which is misleading or information which is false or misleading. In the same spirit he must be watchful to avoid the use, even by accident, of practices or methods incompatible with this Code.

Clause 4

PR activities must be carried out openly: they must be readily identifiable, bear a clear indication of their origin, and must not tend to mislead third parties.

Clause 5

In his relations with other professions and with other branches of social communications, the pr practitioner must respect the rules and practices appropriate to those professions or occupations, so far as these are compatible with the ethics of his own profession.

Section 3 - Specific professional obligations: Towards clients or employers

Clause 6

A pr practitioner shall not represent conflicting or competing interests without the express consent of the clients or employers concerned.

Clause 7

In the practice of his profession, a pr practitioner must observe complete discretion. He must scrupulously respect professional confidence, and in particular must not reveal any confidential information received from his clients or employers, past, present of potential, or make use of such information, without express authorization.

Clause 8

A pr practitioner who has an interest which may conflict with that of his client or employer must disclose it as soon as possible.

Clause 9

A pr practitioner must not recommend to his client or employer the services of any business or organisation in which he has a financial, commercial or other interest without first disclosing that interest.

Clause 10

A pr practitioner shall not enter a contract with his client or employer under which the practitioner guarantees quantified results.

Clause 11

A pr practitioner may accept remuneration for his services only in the form of salary or fees, and on no account may he accept payment or other material rewards contingent upon quantitative results.

Clause 12

A pr practitioner shall not accept for his services to a client or an employer any remuneration from a third party, such as discounts, commissions or payments in kind, except with the agreement of the client or employer.

Clause 13

When the execution of a pr assignment would be likely to entail serious professional misconduct and imply behaviour contrary to the principles of this Code, the pr practitioner must take steps to notify his client or employer immediately, and do everything possible to see that the latter respects the requirements of the Code. If the client or employer persists in his intentions, the practitioner must nevertheless observe the Code irrespective of the consequences to him.

Section 4 Towards public opinion and the information media

Clause 14

The spirit of this Code and the rules contained in preceding clauses, notably clauses 2, 3, 4 and 5 imply a constant concern on the part of the pr practitioner with the right to information, and moreover the duty to provide information, within the limits of professional confidence. They imply also a respect for the rights, independence and initiative of the information media.

Clause 15

Any attempt to deceive public opinion or its representatives is strictly forbidden. Any form of blackmail, corruption or exertion of undue influence, especially in relation to the information media, is forbidden. News must be provided without charge and with no private understanding or hidden reward for its use or publication.

Clause 16

If it should seem neccssary to maintain the initiative in, and the control of, the issue and distribution of information, within the principles of this Code, the pr practitioner may buy space or broadcasting time in conformity with the rules, practices and usages in that field.

Section 5 Towards fellow-practitioners

Clause 17

The pr practitioner must refrain from unfair competition with fellow-practitioners. He must neither act nor speak in a way which could tend to depreciate the reputation or business of a fellow-practitioner, subject always to his duty under Clause 19b of this Code.

Section 6 Towards the profession

Clause 18

The pr practitioner must refrain from any conduct which may prejudice the reputation of his profession. In particular he must not cause harm to his national association, its efficient working, or its good name, whether by malicious attacks or by any breach of its constitution or rules.

The reputation of the profession is the responsibility of each of its members. The pr practitioner has a duty not only to respect this Code himself but also:

a. to assist in making the Code more widely and better known and understood;

b. to report to the competent disciplinary authorities any breach of the Code which comes to his notice, c. to take any action in his power to ensure that rulings on its application by such authorities are observed and sanctions made effective.

Any practitioner who permits a violation of the Code will be considered as having himself breached the Code.

(Reproduced with the kind permission of the Public Relations Institute of Ireland)

APPENDIX 2

International Public Relations Association Code of Conduct (adopted in Venice – May 1961)

A Personal and Professional Integrity. It is understood that by personal integrity is meant the maintenance of both high moral standards and a sound reputation. By professional integrity is meant observance of the Constitution rules and, particularly, the Code as adopted by IPRA.

B Conduct towards Clients and Employers. A member has a general duty of fair dealing towards his/her clients or employers, past and present. A member shall not represent conflicting or competing interests without the express consent of those concerned. A member shall safeguard the confidences of both present and former clients or employers. A member shall not employ methods tending to be derogatory of another member's client or employer. In performing services for a client or employer a member shall not accept fees, commission or any other valuable consideration in connection with those services from anyone other than his/her client or employer without the express consent of his/her client or employer, given after a full disclosure of the facts. A member shall not propose to a prospective client that his/her fees or other compensation be contingent on the achievement of certain results; nor shall he/she enter into any fee agreement to the same effect.

C Conduct towards the Public and the Media. A member shall conduct his/her professional activities with respect to the public interest and for the dignity of the individual. A member shall not engage in practice which tends to corrupt the integrity of channels of public communication. A member shall not intentionally disseminate false or misleading information. A member shall at all times seek to give a faithful representation of the organisation which he/she serves. A member shall not create any organisation to serve some announced cause but actually to serve an undisclosed special or private interest of a member or his/her client or employer, nor shall he/she make use of it or any such existing organisation.

D Conduct towards Colleagues. A member shall not intentionally injure the professional reputation or practice of another member. However, if a member has evidence that another member has been guilty of unethical, illegal or unfair practices, including practices in violation of this Code, he/she should present the information to the Council of IPRA. A member shall not seek to supplant another member with his employer or client. A member shall co-operate with fellow members in upholding and enforcing this Code.

International Code of Ethics (Code of Athens)

CONSIDERING that all Member countries of the United Nations Organisation have agreed to abide by its Charter which reaffirms "its faith in fundamental human rights, in the dignity and worth of the human person" and that having regard to the very nature of the profession, Public Relations practitioners in these countries should undertake to ascertain and observe the principles set out in this Charter;

CONSIDERING that, apart from "rights", human beings have not only physical or material needs but also intellectual, moral and social needs, and that their rights are of real benefit to them only insofar as these needs are essentially met;

CONSIDERING that, in the course of their professional duties and depending on how these duties are performed, Public Relations practitioners can substantially help to meet these intellectual, moral and social needs;

And lastly, CONSIDERING that the use of the techniques enabling them to come simultaneously into contact with millions of people gives Public Relations practitioners a power that has to be restrained by the observance of a strict moral code.

On all these grounds, all members of the International Public Relations Association agree to abide by this International Code of Ethics, and that if, in the light of evidence submitted to the Council, a member should be found to have infringed this Code in the course of his/her professional duties, he/she will be deemed to be guilty of serious misconduct calling for an appropriate penalty.

Accordingly, each member:

SHALL ENDEAVOUR

1. To contribute to the achievement of the moral and cultural conditions enabling human beings to reach their full stature and enjoy the indefeasible rights to which they are entitled under the "Universal declaration of Human Rights";

2. To establish communications patterns and channels which, by fostering the free flow of essential information, will make each member of the group feel that he/she is being kept informed, and also give him/her an awareness of his/her own personal involvement and responsibility, and of his/ her solidarity with other members;

3. To conduct himself/herself always and in all circumstances in such a manner as to deserve and secure the confidence of those with whom he/she comes into contact;

4. To bear in mind that, because of the relationship between his/her profession and the public, his/her conduct - even in private - will have an impact on the way in which the profession as a whole is appraised;

SHALL UNDERTAKE

5. To observe in his/her professional duties, the moral principles and rules of the "Universal Declaration of Human Rights";

6. To pay due regard to, and uphold human dignity and to recognise the right of each individual to judge for himself/herself;

7. To establish the moral, psychological and intellectual conditions for dialogue in its true sense, and to recognise the rights of these parties involved to state their case and express their views;

8. To act, in all circumstances, in such a manner as to take account of the respective interests of the parties involved; both the interests of the orga- nisation which he/she serves and the interests of the publics concerned;

9. To carry out his/her undertakings and commitments which shall always be so worded as to avoid any misunderstanding, and to show loyalty and integrity in all circumstances so as to keep the confidence or his/ her clients or employers, past or present, and all of the publics that are affected by his/her actions;

SHALL REFRAIN FROM

10. Subordinating the truth to other requirements;

11. Circulating information which is not based on established and ascertainable facts;

12. Taking part in any venture or undertaking which is unethical or dishonest or capable of impairing human dignity or integrity;

13. Using any "manipulative" methods or techniques designed to create subconscious motivations which the individual cannot control of his/her own free will and so cannot be held accountable for the action taken on them.

(*Reproduced with the kind permission of the International Public Relations Association, London*)

Appendix 3

Code Of Professional Practice For Public Affairs & Lobbying

(Adopted by the 20th annual general meeting of members of the Public Relations Institute of Ireland held in Dublin on December 8, 2003)

The Public Relations Institute of Ireland (PRII) believes that professional public affairs practice and lobbying are proper, legitimate and important activities, which ensure an open two-way communication between national and local government (including the Oireachtas, the entire public service, as well as other bodies funded wholly or mainly from public funds), the institutions of the European Union (EU) and bodies whose activities and interests are governed, regulated, impacted or otherwise influenced by such institutions. Furthermore, PRII believes that the existence of a defined code for the practice of public affairs and lobbying will serve to enhance the integrity of the democratic process.

Public relations practitioners will, from time to time, make representations to public representatives of all types, whether elected, co-opted, appointed, public servants, those employed in the public service, or those appointed to public bodies (for the purposes of this Code all such people will henceforth be referred to as public officials).

In order to ensure that the activities of its members are conducted to the highest possible standards of practice and ethics, the Public Relations Institute of Ireland has adopted this Code of Professional Practice, which is a condition of membership of the Institute.

The code will direct PRII members as to acceptable and appropriate standards of behaviour in public affairs activity. It complements the obligations of public officials under the Ethics in Public Office Acts, Local Government Acts, Electoral Acts and standard terms of employment and other rules which also govern the activities of such officials.

For the purposes of this Code of Professional Practice, public affairs practice is defined as:

All activity associated with representing the interests of a client or employer in relation to any matter of public policy, including:

- Provision of professional advice to clients/employers on matters relevant to public policy or law; or procurement, selection, nomination or appointment for public contract or office

- Lawful and ethical actions intended to promote a change of public policy or law;
- The making of representations, or the advocacy of a point of view, to any persons or institutions, including the provision of information and advice.

Code of Professional Practice

All members of the Public Relations Institute of Ireland:

A. Conduct towards the public

1 Shall at all times be familiar with and observe all relevant EU, local, national and international law in force, shall have due regard for the public interest and shall not seek to improperly influence the decision-making processes of government, whether local or national, or the E.U. Institutions.

2 Shall take reasonable steps to ensure that all information supplied, and representations made, by them to third parties is factually accurate and honest.

3 Will actively disclose, at the earliest possible opportunity, the identity of clients on whose behalf they are making representations on matters of public policy or decision-making, current or proposed legislation, or in respect of the business of the Oireachtas, Northern Ireland Assembly, local authorities, the European Parliament or any other parliament or legislative assembly.

4 Shall ensure that any financial relationships involved in their professional dealings are legal and ethical. PRII members will neither offer or give, nor cause a client/employer to offer or give, any inducement or reward, direct or indirect, to any public official or person acting on their account.

5 Shall act at all times in a professional, ethical and reasonable manner and shall not bring unreasonable or undue pressure or influence to bear in their activities as public affairs practitioners. All public officials should, at all times, be treated with courtesy and respect.

6 Where he/she is a member of a local authority or is appointed by the government to any state or semi-state body, or is engaged by such organisations on a consultancy basis, shall not offer public affairs consultancy services to third parties in respect of the business or related activities of that authority, body or organisation as well as to related, linked or subsidiary organisations.

7 Shall not offer public affairs consultancy services and simultaneously be a member of the Oireachtas, Northern Ireland Assembly, UK Parliament, European Parliament, or other parliaments or legislative assemblies.

8 Shall not offer public affairs consultancy services for financial reward or other inducements and simultaneously be employed in the Public Service or engaged as a full time advisor to government.

9 Shall, while attending any parliamentary or other representative assembly, national or local government building, observe the rules and procedures of that institution.

B. Conduct towards clients / employers

1 Recognise their duty of professional care to their clients and/or employers.

2 Shall take all necessary steps to ensure that they are properly informed of their clients' or employers' relevant concerns and interests and shall at all times properly and honestly represent these interests.

3 Shall properly inform clients about any potential conflicts of interest, or of any competing interests arising from their professional practice or other business, family or social associations. If it should emerge that an actual conflict of interest exists and it cannot be resolved, the member must cease to act for that client. A member may represent such competing interests only:

> a where he/she has obtained the explicit and informed consent of all the parties involved, and;
>
> b where the member is enabled to act for each of the parties with an equal professionalism and duty of care.

4 Shall, in all cases where any conflict of interest or potential conflict arises between their professional duties and their personal activities, give precedence to their professional responsibilities and where necessary either cease the relevant personal activity or withdraw from their professional duty.

5 Have a positive duty in all their professional dealings to maintain full and proper client confidentiality.

6 Where he/she forms the opinion that the objectives or activities of his or her client/employer may be unethical, illegal or contrary to good professional practice, including this code of conduct, are required to so advise the client/employer. In circumstances where this advice is not acted upon in the appropriate manner, the member shall forthwith cease to act on behalf of the client/employer in such matters.

7 Shall not make improper claims regarding their access to, or influence over any institution of the European Union, national or local government, public official or member of the media.

8 Shall not knowingly guarantee the achievement of results nor undertake assignments which are beyond the member's capabilities.

C. Conduct towards the profession

1 Reaffirm their commitment to the European Code of Professional Practice (Code of Lisbon) and the International Code of Ethics (Code of Athens) and their successors.

2 Shall not bring professional public affairs and public relations practice into disrepute.

Breaches of the Code

Breaches of this Code of Conduct shall be treated as breaches of the Disciplinary Code of the Public Relations Institute of Ireland and shall be subject to such procedures and sanctions as provided for in the Disciplinary Code.

Revisions

The Council of the Public Relations Institute of Ireland may from time to time propose amendments to the code as outlined to members in the event of any further legislative or relevant other developments that in the Council's opinion might require such a change in the interests of its members and in the spirit of the code.

(Reproduced with the kind permission of the Public Relations Institute of Ireland).

APPENDIX 4

The General Rules of the Advertising Standards Authority of Ireland

Principles

2.1 All advertisements should be legal, decent, honest and truthful.

2.2 All advertisements should be prepared with a sense of responsibility to consumers and to society.

2.3 All advertisements should respect the principles of fair competition generally accepted in business.

2.4 The Code is applied in the spirit as well as in the letter.

2.5 An advertisement should not bring advertising into disrepute.

2.6 Primary responsibility for observing the Code rests with advertisers. Others involved in the preparation and publication of advertisements such as agencies and media also accept an obligation to abide by the Code.

2.7 Any unreasonable delay in responding to ASAI's enquiries may be considered a breach of the Code.

2.8 The Authority will observe requests to treat any confidential material supplied in strict confidence unless the Courts or an official agency acting within its statutory powers compel its disclosure.

Substantiation

2.9 Before offering an advertisement for publication, advertisers should be able to provide documentary evidence to substantiate all claims, whether direct or implied, that are capable of objective assessment. Relevant evidence should be sent without delay if requested by the Authority and should be adequate to support both detailed claims and the overall impression created by the advertisement.

2.10 If there is a significant division of informed opinion about any claim made in an advertisement it should not be portrayed as universally accepted.

2.11 Advertisements should not exaggerate the value, accuracy or usefulness of claims contained in books, tapes, videos and the like that have not been independently substantiated.

Legality

2.12 Advertisers have primary responsibility for ensuring that their advertisements are legal. An advertisement should not contain anything that breaks the law or incites anyone to break it, nor omit anything that the law requires.

Decency and Propriety

2.13 An advertisement should contain nothing that is likely to cause grave or widespread offence.

2.14 Advertisements should respect the dignity of all persons and should avoid causing offence on grounds of gender, marital status, family status, sexual orientation, religion, age, disability, race or membership of the traveller community.

2.15 Advertisements should respect the principle of the equality of men and women. They should avoid sex stereotyping and any exploitation or demeaning of men and women. Where appropriate, advertisements should use generic terms that include both the masculine and feminine gender; for example, the term 'business executive' covers both men and women.

2.16 To avoid causing offence, advertisements should be responsive to the diversity in Irish society and advertisements which portray or refer to people within the groups mentioned in **2.14** should:

a. respect the principle of equality in any depiction of these groups;

b. fully respect their dignity and not subject them to ridicule or offensive humour;

c. avoid stereotyping and negative or hurtful images;

d. not exploit them for unrelated commercial purposes;

e. not ridicule or exploit religious beliefs, symbols, rites or practices.

2.17 Advertisers should take account of public sensitivities in the preparation and publication of advertisements and avoid the exploitation of sexuality and the use of coarseness and undesirable innuendo. They should not use offensive or provocative copy or images merely to attract attention.

2.18 The fact that a product is offensive to some people is not in itself sufficient basis for objecting to an advertisement for the product. Advertisers should nevertheless avoid causing offence in such advertisements.

2.19 Compliance with the Code is assessed on the basis of the standards of taste, decency and propriety generally accepted in Ireland, taking account of the product involved, the media used, the location and context in which the advertisement is placed and the characteristics of the audience addressed.

Honesty

2.20 Advertisers should not exploit the credulity, inexperience or lack of knowledge of consumers.

2.21 The design and presentation of advertisements should allow them to be easily and clearly understood. Where footnotes are used they should be of sufficient size and prominence and easily legible; where appropriate they should be linked to the relevant part of the main copy.

Truthfulness

2.22 An advertisement should not mislead by inaccuracy, ambiguity, exaggeration, omission or otherwise.

2.23 Obvious untruths or deliberate hyperbole that are unlikely to mislead, incidental minor inaccuracies and unorthodox spellings are not necessarily in conflict with the Code provided they do not affect the accuracy or perception of the advertisement in any material way.

2.24 Claims such as 'Up to' and 'From' should not exaggerate the value or the range of benefits likely to be achieved in practice by consumers.

Matters of Opinion

2.25 Advertisers may state an opinion about the quality or desirability of a product provided it is clear that what they are expressing is their own opinion rather than a matter of fact and that there is no likelihood of consumers being misled about any matter that is capable of objective assessment. Assertions or comparisons that go beyond subjective opinions are subject to substantiation.

Fear and Distress

2.26 An advertisement should not cause fear or distress without good reason such as the encouragement of prudent behaviour or the discouragement of dangerous or ill-advised actions. In such cases the fear aroused should not be disproportionate to the risk.

Safety

2.27 An advertisement should not encourage dangerous behaviour or show unsafe practices except in the context of promoting safety. Particular care should be taken with advertisements directed at or depicting children.

Violence and Anti-Social Behaviour

2.28 An advertisement should contain nothing that condones or is likely to provoke violence or anti-social behaviour.

Protection of Privacy

2.29 Subject to the exceptions referred to in 2.30 below, advertisers should have written permission in advance from anyone portrayed or referred to in an advertisement. Permission is also required before anyone's house or other possessions can be featured in a manner which identifies the owner to the public.

2.30 Exceptions include the use of crowd scenes or property depicted in general outdoor locations or where the purpose of the advertisement is to promote a product such as a book or film of which the person concerned is a subject.

2.31 Advertisements should not exploit the public reputation of persons in a manner which is humiliating or offensive. Advertisements should not claim or imply an endorsement where none exists. Advertisers are reminded that persons who do not wish to be associated with the advertised product may take legal action against them.

2.32 References to deceased persons should be handled with particular care to avoid causing offence or distress.

Testimonials and Endorsements

2.33 Advertisers who use testimonials should be able to provide relevant supporting documentation to ASAI and they should hold signed and dated proof for any testimonials they use. Testimonials by persons named or depicted in an advertisement may be used only with the prior permission of those persons.

2.34 Testimonials may be misleading if the formulation of the product or its market environment changes significantly. They should therefore relate to the product as currently offered.

2.35 Testimonials do not constitute substantiation and the opinions expressed in them should be supported, where necessary, with independent evidence of their accuracy. Claims based on a testimonial should conform with the Code.

2.36 Endorsements by fictitious or historical characters should not be presented as though they were genuine testimonials.

2.37 References to tests, trials, professional endorsements, research facilities and professional journals should be used only with the permission of those concerned. All such tests, trials and endorsements should be signed and dated. Any establishment referred to should be under appropriate professional supervision.

Prices

2.38 If a price is stated in an advertisement, it should relate to the product depicted or specified in the advertisement. Care should be taken to ensure that prices and illustrated products match.

2.39 Except in advertisements addressed exclusively to the trade, prices quoted should normally include VAT and other taxes, duties or inescapable costs to the consumer. Where applicable, the amounts of any other charges such as those arising from the method of purchase or payment should be stated.

2.40 If the price of one product is dependent on the purchase of another, the extent of any commitment required of consumers should be made clear.

Free Offers

2.41 An offer should be described as free only if consumers pay no more than:

a. the current public rate of postage;

b. the actual cost of freight or delivery;

c. the cost, including incidental expenses, of any travel involved if consumers collect the offer.

In all cases consumers' liability for such costs should be made clear and there should be no additional charges for packaging or handling.

2.42 Advertisers should not attempt to recover their costs by reducing the quality or composition, by imposing additional charges or inflating incidental expenses or by increasing the price of any other product that must be purchased as a pre-condition of obtaining a free item.

Availability of Products

2.43 Advertisers should be in a position to meet any reasonable demand created by their advertising. If a product proves to be available in insufficient quantity, advertisers should take immediate action to ensure that any further advertisements are amended or withdrawn.

2.44 Where there is limited availability on some or all of the products advertised, apart from indicating that there may be other terms and conditions which apply, advertisers should not exaggerate the availability of any of those products; should be able to demonstrate that there is a reasonable supply or proportion of each of the various products available.

2.45 Products should not be advertised as a way of gauging possible demand unless the advertisement makes this clear.

2.46 Advertisers should not use the technique of switch selling, where sales staff criticise the advertised product or suggest that it is not available and recommend purchase of a more expensive alternative. Advertisers should not place obstacles in the way of purchasing the product or delivering it promptly.

Comparisons

2.47 Comparisons are permitted in the interests of public information and vigorous competition. They can be explicit or implied and can relate to advertisers' own products or those of their competitors.

2.48 Comparisons should be fair and should be so designed that there is no likelihood of a consumer being misled. The basis of selection should be clear and the elements of comparison should not be unfairly selected in a way that gives the advertisers an artificial advantage.

2.49 A claim that any product is superior to others should only be made where there is clear evidence to support the claim. Wording which implies superior or superlative status such as "number one", "leading", "largest" and the like should be capable of substantiation with market share data or similar proof.

2.50 Advertisers should not unfairly attack or discredit other businesses or their products.

Guarantees

2.51 Where an advertisement refers to a guarantee, the full terms of the guarantee should be available for consumers to inspect before they are committed to purchase. Any substantial limitations (e.g. one year; parts only) should be clearly indicated in the advertisement.

2.52 'Guarantee' when used in a colloquial sense should not cause confusion about consumers' statutory rights.

Exploitation of Goodwill

2.53 Advertisers should not exploit or make unfair use of the goodwill attached to the name, trademark, brand, slogan or advertising campaign of any other person.

Imitation

2.54 An advertisement should not so closely resemble another as to be likely to mislead or cause confusion.

Recognisability

2.55 An advertisement should be designed and presented in such a way that it is immediately apparent that it is an advertisement.

2.56 An advertisement feature, announcement or promotion published in exchange for a payment or other reciprocal arrangement where the content is controlled by the advertiser should comply with the Code. It should also be clearly identified and distinguished from editorial matter.

(Reproduced with the kind permission of the Advertising Standards Authority of Ireland)

Appendix 5

DEFAMATION ACT, 1961

AN ACT TO CONSOLIDATE WITH AMENDMENTS CERTAIN ENACTMENTS RELATING TO THE LAW OF DEFAMATION.
[17th August, 1961]

BE IT ENACTED BY THE OIREACHTAS AS FOLLOWS:—

Short title

1.—This Act may be cited as the Defamation Act, 1961.

Interpretation generally

2.—In this Act—

"**local authority**" has the same meaning as in the Local Government Act, 1941;

"**newspaper**" except in section 27, means any paper containing public news or observations thereon, or consisting wholly or mainly of advertisements, which is printed for sale and is published in the State or in Northern Ireland either periodically or in parts or numbers at intervals not exceeding thirty-six days;

"**proprietor**" means, as well as the sole proprietor of any newspaper, in the case of a divided proprietorship, the persons who, as partners or otherwise, represent or are responsible for any share or interest in the newspaper as between themselves and the persons in like manner representing or responsible for the other shares or interests therein, and no other person.

Commencement and proceedings affected

3.—(1) This Act shall come into operation on the 1st day of January, 1962.

(2) Part III of this Act shall apply for the purposes of any proceedings

begun after the commencement of this Act, whenever the cause of action arose, but shall not affect any proceedings commenced before the commencement of this Act.

Repeals

4.—The enactments specified in the First Schedule to this Act are hereby repealed.

Competence of jury to give general verdict on trial of indictment for libel

5.—(1) On every trial of an indictment for making or publishing any libel to which a plea of not guilty is entered, the jury may give a general verdict of guilty or not guilty upon the whole matter put in issue on the indictment, and the jury shall not be required or directed by the court to find the person charged guilty merely on the proof of the publication by him of the paper charged to be a libel and of the sense ascribed to such paper in the indictment.

(2) On every such trial the court according to its discretion, give its opinion and directions to the jury on the matter in issue in like manner as in other criminal cases.

(3) Subsections (1) and (2) of this section shall not operate to prevent the jury from finding a special verdict, in their discretion, as in other criminal cases.

Plea of truth of matters charged on trial for defamatory libel and that publication was for public benefit

6.—On the trial of any indictment for a defamatory libel, the person charged having pleaded such plea as hereinafter mentioned, the truth of the matters charged may be inquired into but shall not amount to a defence, unless it was for the public benefit that the said matters charged should be published; and to entitle the defendant to give evidence of the truth of such matters charged as a defence to such indictment, it shall be necessary for the person charged in pleading to the said indictment, to allege the truth of the said matters charged, in the manner required in pleading a justification to an action for defamation, and further to allege that it was for the public benefit that the said matters charged should be published, and the particular fact or facts by reason of which it was for the public benefit that the said matters charged should be published, to which plea the prosecutor shall be at liberty to reply generally, denying the whole thereof; and if, after such plea, the person charged is convicted on such indictment, the court may, in pronouncing sentence, consider whether his guilt is aggravated or mitigated by the said plea and by the evidence given to prove or to disprove the same: provided that—

(*a*) the truth of the matters charged in the alleged libel complained of by such indictment shall in no case be inquired into without such plea of justification;
(*b*) in addition to such plea of justification, the person charged may enter a plea of not guilty;
(*c*) nothing in this section shall take away or prejudice any defence under the plea of not guilty which it is competent to the person charged to make under such plea to any indictment for defamatory libel.

Evidence by person charged to rebut prima facie case of publication by his agent

7.—Whenever, upon the trial of an indictment for the publication of a libel, a plea of not guilty having been entered, evidence is given establishing a presumption of publication against the person charged by the act of any other person by his authority, it shall be competent for the person charged to prove that the publication was made without his authority, consent or knowledge and that the publication did not arise from want of due care or caution on his part.

Judge required for prosecution of newspaper proprietor, etc

8.—No criminal prosecution stall be commenced against any proprietor, publisher, editor or any person responsible for the publication of a newspaper for any libel published therein without the order of a Judge of the High Court sitting in camera being first had and obtained, and every application for such order shall be made on notice to the person accused, who shall have an opportunity of being heard against the application.

Inquiry as to libel being for public benefit or being true

9.—A Justice of the District Court, upon the hearing of a charge against a proprietor, publisher or editor or any person responsible for the publication of a newspaper for a libel published therein, may receive evidence as to the publication being for the public benefit, as to the matters charged in the libel being true, as to the report being fair and accurate and published without malice and as to any matter which, under this or any other Act or otherwise, might be given in evidence by way of defence by the person charged on his trial on indictment, and the Justice, if, of opinion after hearing such evidence that there is a strong or probable presumption that the jury on the trial would acquit the person charged, may dismiss the case.

Provisions as to summary conviction for libel

10.—If a Justice of the District Court, upon the hearing of a charge against a proprietor, publisher, editor or any person responsible for the publication of a newspaper for a libel published therein, is of opinion that, though the person charged is shown to have been guilty, the libel was of a trivial character and that the offence may be adequately punished by virtue of the powers conferred by this section, the Justice shall cause the charge to be reduced into writing and read to the person charged and shall then ask him if he desires to be tried by a jury or consents to the case being dealt with summarily, and, if such person consents to the case being dealt with summarily, may summarily convict him, and impose on him a fine not exceeding fifty pounds, and the Summary Jurisdiction Acts shall apply accordingly.

Penalty for maliciously publishing defamatory libel

11.—Every person who maliciously publishes any defamatory libel shall, on conviction thereof on indictment, be liable to a fine not exceeding two hundred pounds or to imprisonment for a term not exceeding one year or to both such fine and imprisonment.

Penalty for maliciously publishing libel known to be false

12.—Every person who maliciously publishes any defamatory libel, knowing the same to be false, shall, on conviction thereof on indictment, be liable to a fine not exceeding five hundred pounds or to imprisonment for a term not exceeding two years or to both such fine and imprisonment.

Penalty for printing or publishing blasphemous or obscene libel

13.—(1) Every person who composes, prints or publishes any blasphemous or obscene libel shall, on conviction thereof on indictment, be liable to a fine not exceeding five hundred pounds or imprisonment for a term not exceeding two years or to both fine and imprisonment or to penal servitude for a term not exceeding seven years.

(*a*) In every case in which a person is convicted of composing, printing or publishing a blasphemous libel, the court may make an order for the seizure and carrying away and detaining in safe custody, in such manner as shall be directed in the order, of all copies of the, libel in the possession of such person or of any other person named in the order for his use, evidence upon oath having been previously given to the satisfaction of the court that copies of the said libel are in the possession of such other person for the use of thc person convicted.

(*b*) Upon the making of an order under paragraph (*a*)of this subsection, any member of the Garda Síochána acting under such order may enter, if necessary by the use of force, and search for any copies of the said libel any building, house or other place belonging to the person convicted or to such other person named in the order and may seize and carry away and detain in the manner directed in such order all copies of the libel found therein.

(*c*) If, in any such case, the conviction is quashed on appeal, any copies of the libel seized under an order under paragraph (*a*)of this subsection shall be returned free of charge to the person or persons from whom they were seized.

(*d*) Where, in any such case, an appeal is not lodged or the conviction is confirmed on appeal, any copies of the libel seized under an order under paragraph (*a*)of this subsection shall, on the application of a member of the Garda Síochána to the court which made such order, be disposed of in such manner as such court may direct.

Interpretation.(Part III)

14.—(1) In this Part—

"**broadcast**" has the same meaning as in the Wireless Telegraphy Act, 1926 (in this section referred to as the Act of 1926) and "broadcasting" shall be construed accordingly;

"**broadcasting station**" has the same meaning as in the Act of 1926, as amended by the Broadcasting Authority Act, 1960;

"**wireless**" telegraphy has the same meaning as in the Act of 1926.

(2) Any reference in this Part to words shall be construed as including a

reference to visual images, gestures and other methods of signifying meaning.

(3) Where words broadcast by means of wireless telegraphy are simultaneously transmitted by telegraph as defined by the Telegraph Act, 1863, in accordance, with a licence granted by the Minister for Posts and Telegraphs, the provisions of this Part shall apply as if the transmission were broadcasting by means of wireless telegraphy.

Broad statements

15.—For the purposes of the law of libel and slander the broadcasting of words by means of wireless telegraphy shall be treated as publication in permanent form.

Words imputing unchastity or adultery actionable out special damage

16.—Words spoken and published which impute unchastity or adultery to any woman or girl shall not require special damage to render them actionable.

Offer of an apology admissible in evidence in mitigation of damages in action for defamation

17.—In any action for defamation, it shall be lawful for the defendant (after notice in writing of his intention so to do, duly given to the plaintiff at the time of filing or delivering the plea in the action) to give in evidence, in mitigation of damage, that he made or offered an apology to the plaintiff for such defamation before the commencement of the action, or as soon as afterwards as he had an opportunity of doing so, in case the action shall have been commenced before there was an opportunity of making or of offering such apology.

Newspaper and broadcast reports of proceedings in court privileged

18.—(1) A fair and accurate report published in any newspaper or broadcast by means of wireless telegraphy as part of any programme or service provided by means of a broadcasting station within the State or in Northern Ireland of proceedings publicly heard before any court established by law and exercising judicial authority within the State or in Northern Ireland shall, if published or broadcast contemporaneously with such proceedings, be privileged.

(2) Nothing in subsection (1) of this section shall authorise the

publication or broadcasting of any blasphemous or obscene matter.

Slander affecting official, professional or business reputation

19.—In an action for slander in respect of words calculated to disparage the plaintiff in any office, profession, calling, trade or business held or carried on by him at the time of the publication, but shall not be necessary to allege or prove special damage, whether or not the words are spoken of the plaintiff in the way of his office, profession, calling, trade or business.

Slander of title, etc

20.—(1) In an action for slander of title, slander of goods or other malicious falsehood, it shall not be necessary to allege or prove special damage—

(*a*) if the words upon which the action is founded are calculated to cause pecuniary damage to the plaintiff and are published in writing or other permanent form; or
(*b*) if the said words calculated to cause pecuniary damage to the plaintiff in respect of any office, profession, calling, trade or business held or carried on by him at the time of the publication.

(2) Section 15 of this Act shall apply for the purposes of subsection (1) of this section as it applies for the purposes of the law of libel and slander.

Unintentional defamation

21.—(1) A person who has published words alleged to be defamatory of another person may, if he claims that the words were published by him innocently in relation to that other person, make an offer of amends under this section, and in any such case—

(*a*) if the offer is accepted by the party aggrieved and is duly performed, no proceedings for libel or slander shall be taken or continued by that party against the person making the offer in respect of the publication in question (but without prejudice to any cause of action against any other person jointly responsible for that publication);
(*b*) if the offer is not accepted by the party aggrieved, then, except as otherwise provided by this section, it shall be a defence, in any proceedings by him for libel or slander against the person making the offer in respect of the publication in question, to

prove that the words complained of were published by the defendant innocently in relation to the plaintiff and that the offer was made as soon as practicable after the defendant received notice that they were or might be defamatory of the plaintiff, and has not been withdrawn.

(2) An offer of amends under this section must be expressed to be made for the purposes of this section, and must be accompanied by an affidavit specifying the facts relied upon by the person making it to show that the words in question were published by him innocently in relation to the party aggrieved; and for the purposes of a defence under paragraph (*b*) of subsection (1) of this section no evidence, other than evidence of facts specified in the affidavit, shall be admissible on behalf of that person to prove that the words were so published.

(3) An offer of amends under this section shall be understood to mean an offer—

(*a*) in any case, to publish or join in the publication of a suitable correction of the words complained of, and a sufficient apology to the party aggrieved in respect of those words;

(*b*) where copies of a document or record containing the said words have been distributed by or with the knowledge of the person making the offer, to take such steps as are reasonably practicable on his part for notifying persons to whom copies have been so distributed that the words are alleged to be defamatory of the party aggrieved.

(4) Where an offer of amends under this section is accepted by the party aggrieved—

(*a*) any question as to the steps to be taken in fulfilment of the offer as so accepted shall, in default of agreement between the parties, be referred to and determined by the High Court or, if proceedings in respect of the publication in question have been taken in the Circuit Court, by the Circuit Court, and the decision of such Court thereon shall be final;

(*b*) the power of the court to make orders as to costs in proceedings by the party aggrieved against the person making the offer in respect of the publication in question, or in proceedings in respect of the offer under paragraph (*a*)of this subsection, shall include power to order the payment by the person making the offer to the party aggrieved of costs on an indemnity basis and any expenses reasonably incurred or to be incurred by that party in consequence of the publication in question;

and if no such proceedings as aforesaid are taken, the High Court may, upon application made by the party aggrieved, make any such order for the payment of such costs and expenses as aforesaid as could be made in such proceedings.

(5) For the purposes of this section words shall be treated as published by one person (in this subsection referred to as the publisher) innocently in relation to another person if, and only if, the following conditions are satisfied, that is to say—

(*a*) that the publisher did not intend to publish them of and concerning that other person, and did not know of circumstances by virtue of which they might be understood to refer to him; or

(*b*) that the words were not defamatory on the face of them, and the publisher did not know of circumstances by virtue of which they might be understood to be defamatory of that other person,

and in either case that the publisher exercised all reasonable in relation to the publication; and any reference in this subsection to the publisher shall be construed as including a reference to any servant or agent of the publisher who was concerned with the contents of the publication—

(6) Paragraph (*b*) of subsection (1) of this section shall not apply where the party aggrieved proves that he has suffered special damage.

(7) Paragraph (*b*) of subsection (1) of this section shall not apply in relation to the publication by any person of words of which he is not the author unless he proves that the words were written by the author without malice.

Justification

22.—In an action for libel or slander in respect of words containing two or more distinct charges against the plaintiff, a defence of justification shall not fail by reason only that the truth of every charge is not proved, if the words not proved to be true do not materially injure the plaintiff's reputation having regard to the truth of the remaining charges.

Fair comment

23.—In an action for libel or slander in respect of words consisting partly of allegations of fact and partly of expression of opinion, a defence of fair comment shall not fail by reason only that the truth of every allegation of fact is not proved, if the expression of opinion is fair comment having regard to such of the facts alleged or referred to in the words complained of as are proved.

Qualified privilege of certain newspaper and broadcasting reports

24.—(1) Subject to the provisions of this section, the publication in a newspaper or the broadcasting by means of wireless telegraphy as part of any programme or service provided by means of a broadcasting station within the State or in Northern Ireland of any such report or other matter as is mentioned in the Second Schedule to this Act shall be privileged unless the publication or broadcasting is proved to be made with malice.

(2) In an action for libel in respect of the publication or broadcasting of any such report or matter as is mentioned in Part II of the Second Schedule to this Act, the provisions of this section shall not be a defence if it is proved that the defendant has been requested by the plaintiff to publish in the newspaper in which the original publication was made or to broadcast from the broadcasting station from which the original broadcast was made, whichever is the case, a reasonable statement by way of explanation or contradiction, and has refused or neglected to do so, or has done so in a manner not adequate or not reasonable having regard to all the circumstances.

(3) Nothing in this section shall be construed as protecting the publication or broadcasting of any matter the publication or broadcasting of which is prohibited by law, or of any matter which is not of public concern and the publication or broadcast of which is not for the public benefit.

(4) Nothing in this section shall be construed as limiting or bridging any privilege subsisting (otherwise than by virtue of section 4 of the Law of Libel Amendment Act, 1888) immediately before the commencement of this Act.

Agreements for indemnity

25.—An agreement for indemnifying any person against civil ability for libel in respect of the publication of any matter shall not be unlawful unless at the time of the publication that person knows that the matter is defamatory, and does not reasonably believe there is a good defence to any action brought upon it.

Evidence of other damages recovered by plaintiff

26.—In any action for libel or slander the defendant may give evidence in mitigation of damages that the plaintiff has recovered damages, or has brought actions for damages, for libel or slander n respect of the publication of words to the same effect as the words on which the action is founded, or has received or agreed to receive compensation in respect of any such publication.

Obligation on certain newspaper proprietors to be registered under the Registration of Business Names Act, 1916

27.—(1) The proprietor of every newspaper having a place of business in the State shall, where such proprietor is not a company registered under the Companies Acts, 1908 to 1959, and is not required under the provisions of the Registration of Business Names Act, 1916, to be registered under that Act in respect of the business of carrying on such newspaper, be registered in the manner directed by that Act, and that Act shall apply to such proprietor in like manner as it applies to a film or individual referred to in section 1 thereof.

(2) Every reference in the Registration of Business Names Act, 1916, to that Act shall be construed as a reference to that Act as extended by subsection (1) of this section.

(3) In this section "newspaper" means any paper containing public news or observations thereon, or consisting wholly or mainly of advertisements, which is printed for sale and is published in the State either periodically or in parts or numbers at intervals not exceeding twenty-six days.

Saving

28.—Nothing in this Parts hall affect the law relating to criminal libel.

First Schedule

SECTION 4.

Enactments Repealed

PART I: Acts of the Parliament of Ireland

28 Hen.8, c.7 (Ir.): An Act of Slaunder

2 Geo.1, c.20 (Ir.): An Act to limit the time for Criminal Prosecutions for words spoken

33 Geo.3, c.43 (Ir.): An Act to remove doubts respecting the functions of juries in cases of libel

PART II: Acts of the Parliament of the late United Kingdom of Great Britain and Ireland

60 Geo.3 & 1 Geo.4, c.8:Criminal Libel Act, 1819

3 & 4 Vic., c.9: Parliamentary Papers Act, 1840.

6 & 7 Vic., c.96: Libel Act, 1843.

8 & 9 Vic., c.75: Libel Act, 1845.

32 & 33 Vic., c.24. Newspapers Printers and Reading Rooms Repeal Act, 1869.

44 & 45 Vic., c.60. Newspaper Libel and Registration Act, 1881.

51 & 52 Vic., c.64. Law of Libel Amendment Act, 1888.

54 & 55 Vic., c.51. Slander of Women Act, 1891. Section 24.

Second Schedule

SECTION 24.

STATEMENTS HAVING QUALIFIED PRIVILEGE

PART I

Statements privileged without Explanation or Contradiction

1. A fair and accurate report of any proceedings in public of a house of any legislature (including subordinate or federal legislatures) of any foreign sovereign State or any body which is part of such legislature or any body duly appointed by or under the legislature or executive of such State to hold a public inquiry in a matter of public importance.
2. A fair and accurate report of any proceedings in public of an international organization of which the State or the Government as a member or of any international conference to which the Government sends a representative.

3. A fair and accurate report of any proceedings in public of the International Court of Justice and any other judicial or arbitral tribunal deciding matters in dispute between States.

4. A fair and accurate report of any proceedings before a court (including a court-martial) exercising jurisdiction under the law of any legislature (including subordinate or federal legislatures) of any foreign sovereign State.

5. A fair and accurate copy of or extract from any register kept in pursuance of any law which is open to inspection by the public or of any other document which is required by law to be open to inspection by the public.

6. Any notice or advertisement published by or on the authority of any court in the State or in Northern Ireland or any Judge or officer of such a court.

PART II

Statements privileged subject to Explanation or Contradiction

1. A fair and accurate report of the findings, or decision of any of the following associations, whether formed in the State or Northern Ireland, or of any committee or governing body thereof, that is to say

    (*a*) an association for the purpose of promoting or encouraging the exercise of or interest in any art, science, religion or learning, and empowered by its constitution to exercise control over or adjudicate upon matters of interest or concern to the association or the actions or conduct of any persons subject to such control or adjudication;

    (*b*) an association for the purpose of promoting or safe, guarding the interests of any trade, business, industry or profession or of the persons carrying on or engaged in any trade, by industry or profession and empowered by its constitution to exercise control over or adjudicate upon matters connected with the trade, business, industry or profession or the actions or conduct of those persons;

    (*c*) an association for the purpose of promoting or safeguarding the interests of any game, sport or pastime, to the playing or exercise of which members of the public are invited or admitted, and empowered by its constitution to exercise control over or adjudicate upon persons connected with or taking part in the game, sport or pastime;

being a finding or decision relating to a person who is a member of or is subject by virtue of any contract to the control of the association.

2. A fair and accurate report of the proceedings at any public meeting held in the State or Northern Ireland, being a meeting *bona fide* and lawfully held for a lawful purpose and for the furtherance or discussion of any matter of public concern whether the admission to the meeting is general or restricted.

3. A fair and accurate report of the proceedings at any meeting or sitting of—

(*a*) any local authority, or committee of a long authority or local authorities, and any corresponding authority, or committee thereof in Northern Ireland;

(*b*) any Judge or Justice acting otherwise than as a court exercising judicial authority and any corresponding person so acting in Northern Ireland;

(*c*) any commission, tribunal, committee or person appointed, whether in the State or Northern Ireland, for the purposes of any inquiry under statutory authority;

(*d*) any person appointed by a local authority to hold a local inquiry in pursuance of an Act of the Oireachtas and any person appointed by a corresponding authority in Northern Ireland to hold a local inquiry in pursuance of statutory authority;

(*e*) any other tribunal, board, committee or body constituted by or under, and exercising functions under, statutory authority, whether in the State or Northern Ireland;

not being a meeting or sitting admission to which is not allowed to representatives of the press and other members of the public.

4. A fair and accurate report of the proceedings at a general meeting, whether in the State or Northern Ireland, of any company or association constituted, registered or certified by or under statutory authority or

incorporated by charter, not being, in the case of a company in the State, a private company within the meaning of the Companies Acts, 1908 to 1959, or, in the case of a company in Northern Ireland, a private company within the meaning of the statutes relating to companies for the time being in force therein.

5. A copy or fair and accurate report or summary of any notice or other matter issued for the information of the public by or on behalf of any Government department, local authority or the Commissioner of the Garda Síochána or by or on behalf of a corresponding department, authority or officer in Northern Ireland.

(Source: Irish Statute Book Database © Government of Ireland. Oireachtas Copyright Material is reproduced with the permission of the Houses of the Oireachtas)

APPENDIX 6

AN BILLE UM PRÍOBHÁIDEACHT 2006

PRIVACY BILL 2006

Mar a tionscnaíodh
As initiated

ARRANGEMENT OF SECTIONS

Section

ACTS REFERRED TO

Broadcasting Act 2001	2001, No. 4
Civil Liability Act 1961	1961, No. 41
Courts (Supplemental Provisions) Act 1961	1961, No. 39
Data Protection Acts 1988 and 2003	
Freedom of Information Act 1997	1997, No. 13
Local Government Act 2001	2001, No. 37
Non-Fatal Offences Against the Person Act 1997	1997, No. 26
Statute of Limitations 1957	1957, No. 6

AN BILLE UM PRÍOBHÁIDEACHT 2006

PRIVACY BILL 2006

BILL

entitled

AN ACT TO PROVIDE FOR A TORT OF VIOLATION OF PRIVACY; AND TO PROVIDE FOR MATTERS CONNECTED THEREWITH.

BE IT ENACTED BY THE OIREACHTAS AS FOLLOWS:

Definitions.

1.—In this Act—
"act" includes disclosure;
"Act of 1957" means the Statute of Limitations 1957;
"disclosure" means, in relation to information, documentation or other material concerning an individual, disclosure of that information, documentation or material to the public or a section of the public, and cognate words shall be construed accordingly;
"individual" means a person other than a body corporate;
"local authority" has the same meaning as it has in the Local Government Act 2001;
"plaintiff" includes a defendant counterclaiming in respect of a violation of privacy;
"privacy action" means an action for an order under *section 8* for violation of privacy;
"public body" has the same meaning as it has in the Freedom of Information Act 1997;
"public place" means any place to which members of the public have access whether as of right or by permission, and whether subject to or free of charge;
"public servant" means—

- (*a*) a civil servant of the State or a civil servant of the Government,
- (*b*) a person who holds a position in any body established by or under an enactment,
- (*c*) a person duly appointed—
  - (i) by a Minister of the Government, the Government, either House of the Oireachtas or a court

established by law, or

(ii) under an enactment,

to conduct an inquiry or investigation in relation to any matter,

(*d*) a person who holds a position in a local authority,

(*e*) a member of the Garda Síochána,

(*f*) a member of the Defence Forces;

"surveillance" includes, in relation to an individual—

(*a*) aural or visual surveillance of that individual,

(*b*) eavesdropping on, watching, spying on, besetting or following that individual,

(*c*) the interception or recording by any person of a communication from an individual to another person by any means (whether electronic or otherwise),

(*d*) the recording by any means of a conversation between 2 or more individuals without the knowledge of one or more of those individuals by any person including one of 20 those individuals,

whether or not effected by trespassing on the property of another.

Tort of violation of privacy.

2.—(1) A person who, wilfully and without lawful authority, violates the privacy of an individual commits a tort (to be known, and in this Act referred to, as the "tort of violation of privacy").

(2) The tort of violation of privacy is actionable without proof of special damage.

Entitlement to privacy.

3.—(1) For the purposes of this section, the privacy to which an individual is entitled is that which is reasonable in all the circumstances having regard to the rights of others and to the requirements of public order, public morality and the common good.

(2) Without prejudice to the generality of *subsection* (*1*) and subject to *sections* 5 and 6, it shall be a violation of the privacy of an individual for a person—

(*a*) to subject an individual to surveillance,

(*b*) to disclose information, documentation or material obtained by surveillance whether or not such surveillance was carried out by or on behalf of the person disclosing such information,

(*c*) to use the name, likeness or voice of the individual, without the consent of that individual, for the purpose of—

(i) advertising or promoting the sale of, or trade in, any property or service, or

(ii) financial gain to the said person,

if, in the course of such use, the individual concerned is identified or, as a result of such use, is capable of being identified, and the said person knew that that individual had not given such consent,

(*d*) to disclose letters, diaries, medical records or other documents concerning the individual or information obtained therefrom, or

(*e*) to commit an act described in section 10 of the Non-Fatal Offences Against the Person Act 1997.

Matters to which court shall have regard.

4.—(1) The court in a privacy action shall, in determining whether an act of a person constitutes a violation of the privacy of an individual, have regard to the nature of the act concerned and all of the relevant circumstances, including—

(*a*) the place where, and the occasion on which, the act was committed,

(*b*) the age of the individual,

(*c*) any office or position (whether of emolument or not) held by the individual and any functions performable by the individual by virtue of his or her holding that office or position, and the extent (if any) to which the act pertains to that office or position or any or all of those functions,

(*d*) the purpose for which information, documentation or other material (if any) obtained as a result of the act was, or was intended to be, used,

(*e*) whether the person, in doing the act, intentionally or recklessly trespassed on the property of another, and

(*f*) whether the person, in doing the act, committed an offence.

(2) Without prejudice to the generality of *subsection* (*1*), the court in a privacy action shall, in determining whether a disclosure concerning an individual is a violation of the privacy of the individual, have regard to the nature of the disclosure and all other relevant circumstances, including—

(*a*) whether the disclosure—

(i) consists in whole or in part of sensitive or intimate private facts concerning the individual,

(ii) concerns the individual's private, home or family life, or

(iii) is in contravention of a duty of a public body not to disclose information, documentation or material of a class to which the disclosure relates,

(*b*) the manner of the disclosure, and

(*c*) the extent of the disclosure.

(3) The claim of a plaintiff in a privacy action brought in respect of a disclosure shall not be defeated by reason only of the defendant's proving that the disclosure consisted of information—

(*a*) that, at the time of the disclosure, was contained in a register or other similar document to which members of the public or a section of the public had access,

(*b*) that the plaintiff had already disclosed to members of his or her family or to his or her friends, or

(*c*) that, subject to *section 6*(*b*), had already been disclosed by a person other than the defendant without the consent of the plaintiff.

(4) The claim of a plaintiff in a privacy action brought in respect of a disclosure shall not be defeated by reason only of the defendant's proving that the disclosure related to an event or occurrence that happened in a public place or a place that, at the time of the disclosure, was visible to members of the public.

Defences.

5.—(1) It shall be a defence to a privacy action for the defendant to prove that the act in respect of which the action was brought—

(*a*) was done for the purpose of lawfully defending or protecting a person or property (including the prosecution or defence of proceedings either civil or criminal),

(*b*) was authorised or required by law or by a court or process of a court established by law,

(*c*) was done by a public servant—

(i) acting in the course of his or her duties, or

(ii) in circumstances where he or she had reasonable grounds for believing that he or she was acting in the course of his or her duties, or

(*d*) consisted of the installation or operation, in good faith, of a closed circuit television system or other surveillance system—

(i) for a purpose authorised by law, or

(ii) for the purpose of detecting or preventing the commission of an offence or the protection of persons or property,

(*e*) was an act of newsgathering, provided any disclosure of material obtained as a result of such act was—
  (i) done in good faith,
  (ii) for the purpose of discussing a subject of public importance,
  (iii) for the public benefit, and
  (iv) fair and reasonable in all of the circumstances.

(2) In this section—

"act of newsgathering" means an act that is reasonable in all of the circumstances and that consists of, or is necessary or incidental to—

(*a*) the acquisition or preparation of material for publication in a periodical, or

(*b*) the acquisition or preparation of material for broadcasting.

"broadcasting" shall be construed in accordance with the Broadcasting Act 2001;

"periodical" means any newspaper, magazine, journal or other publication that is printed, published or issued, or that circulates, in the State at regular or substantially regular intervals and includes any version thereof published, in whole or in part, on the internet or by other electronic means.

Certain disclosures not a violation of privacy.

6.—Disclosure by a person of any information, documentation or other material concerning an individual is not a violation of privacy where—

(*a*) the disclosure was done in good faith and was—
  (i) for the purpose of discussing a subject of public importance,
  (ii) for the public benefit, and
  (iii) fair and reasonable in all of the circumstances,

(*b*) it is obtained by another person in violation of the privacy of the individual and was later disclosed in good faith by the first-mentioned person in circumstances where at the time of disclosure—
  (i) he or she had no knowledge of, and
  (ii) there existed no reasonable grounds for his or her believing, that it had been so obtained,

(*c*) the disclosure is of a statement to which the defence of absolute privilege or defence of qualified privilege under the law of defamation would apply,

(*d*) the disclosure is made by a public servant—
  (i) acting in the course of his or her duties, or
  (ii) in circumstances where he or she had reasonable grounds for believing that he or she was acting in the course of his or her duties, or

(*e*) it consists of the disclosure of personal data within the meaning of the Data Protection Acts 1988 and 2003 other than in contravention of those Acts.

Jurisdiction of courts.

7.—(1) A privacy action may be brought in the High Court or Circuit Court.

(2) The Third Schedule to the Courts (Supplemental Provisions) Act 1961 is amended by the insertion of the following:

"

7B.	A privacy action within the meaning of the *Privacy Act 2006*	Where the amount of the claim exceeds €50,000	At the election of the plaintiff— (*a*) the judge of the circuit where the tort is alleged to have been committed, or (*b*) the judge of the circuit where the defendants or one of the defendants resides or carries on business.

".

Remedies.

8.—(1) The court in a privacy action may—

(*a*) make an order prohibiting the doing by the defendant of any act that it considers would violate the privacy of the plaintiff,

(*b*) order the defendant to pay such damages (if any) to the plaintiff as the court considers appropriate,

(*c*) order the defendant to pay to the plaintiff damages equal to any, or any likely, financial gain accruing to the defendant as a result of the violation of the plaintiff's privacy,

(*d*) order the defendant to deliver to the plaintiff any documents, articles, photographs or other material, and all copies thereof, concerning the plaintiff or belonging to the plaintiff that are in the possession or procurement of the defendant and that were obtained or made as a result of the violation of the plaintiff's privacy.

(2) The court in a privacy action may, in addition to any order under

subsection (*1*), grant to the plaintiff such other relief as in all the circumstances of the case it considers appropriate.

(3) The court in a privacy action may make such order as to costs as it considers appropriate.

(4) The court in a privacy action may make an award of aggravated, or exemplary or punitive, damages as if the cause of action to which the action relates were a cause of action at common law.

Dismissal for want of prosecution.

9.—(1) Where rules of court provide that the plaintiff in a privacy action is, not later than one year from the bringing of the privacy action, required to do any thing and the plaintiff fails to so do, the defendant may, upon the expiration of that period, apply to the court to have the action dismissed, and the court shall dismiss the action upon such application unless the dismissal of the action would result in injustice being done.

(2) An application under this section shall be brought by motion on notice to the plaintiff.

Appeals in privacy actions.

10.—Upon the hearing of an appeal from a decision of the High Court in a privacy action, the Supreme Court may, in addition to any other order that it deems appropriate to make, substitute for any amount of damages awarded to the plaintiff by the High Court such amount as it considers appropriate.

Limitation of action.

11.—(1) Section 11 of the Act of 1957 is amended—

(*a*) in subsection (2), by—

(i) the substitution, in paragraph (*a*), of the words "Subject to paragraphs (*b*), (*c*), and (*d*) of this subsection" for the words "Subject to paragraphs (*b*), and (*c*)of this subsection", and

(ii) the insertion of the following paragraphs:

"(*d*) A privacy action within the meaning of the *Privacy Act 2006* shall not be brought after the expiration of—

(i) one year, or

(ii) such longer period as the court may direct not exceeding 2 years,

from the date on which the cause of action accrued.", and

(*b*) the insertion of the following subsections:

"(3C) The court shall not give a direction under subsection (2)(*d*)(ii) (inserted by *section 11*(*1*)(*a*) of the *Privacy Act 2006*) unless it is satisfied that—

(*a*) the interests of justice require the giving of the direction,

(*b*) the prejudice that the plaintiff would suffer if the direction were not given would significantly outweigh the prejudice that the defendant would suffer if the direction were given,

and the court shall, in deciding whether to give such a direction, have regard to the reason for the failure to bring the action within the period specified in subparagraph (i) of the said subsection (2)(*d*) and the extent to which any evidence relevant to the matter is, by virtue of the delay, no longer capable of being adduced.

(3D) For the purposes of the bringing of a privacy action under the *Privacy Act 2006*, the date of accrual of the cause of action shall be the date upon which the violation of privacy was first discovered by the plaintiff or reasonably discoverable by him or her.".

(2) Section 49 of the Act of 1957 is amended by the insertion of the following subsection:

"(3A) In the case of privacy actions within the meaning of the *Privacy Act 2006*, subsection (1) of this section shall have effect as if for the words 'six years' there were substituted the words 'one year or such longer period as the court may direct not exceeding two years.'.".

Notice of intention to bring action.

12.—(1) An individual shall not bring a privacy action unless—

(*a*) before the bringing of the action and before the expiration of 3 months from the date of accurual of the cause of action in accordance with the Act of 1957, he or she infroms, by notice in writing, the person against whom he or she proposes to bring the action of his or her intention to do so, or

(*b*) the court in which he or she intends to bring the action gives its consent to the action being brought without there being compliance with *paragraph* (*a*).

(2) Any period during which a person is under a disability in accordance with the Act of 1957 shall not be reckonable for the purposes of measuring the period of 3 months specified in *subsection* (*1*).

Hearing of action other than in public.

13.—(1) Upon the application of any individual, a court before which any action founded on tort is brought may, for the purpose of protecting the privacy of the individual, order that—

(*a*) the action or any part of the action, including any interim or interlocutory application, shall be heard otherwise than in public,

(*b*) all persons (other than the parties to the proceedings and persons of such a class as the court may specify) should not be present during the action or any part of the action, including any interim or interlocutory application,

(*c*) the identity of the individual shall not be disclosed other than to such person, or person belonging to such class of persons, as may be specified in the order concerned, or

(*d*) there shall be no publication or broadcast of any material likely to lead to the identification of the person.

(2) This section shall not affect any other power of a court to order that—

(*a*) proceedings before it shall be heard otherwise than in public,

(*b*) the identity of any party to those proceedings or to whom those proceedings relate, or any person called as a witness in those proceedings, shall not be disclosed, or

(*c*) there shall be no publication or broadcast of any material likely to lead to the identification of a person referred to in *paragraph* (*b*).

Trial of privacy action.

14.—A privacy action shall be tried without a jury.

Extinguishment of cause of action on death.

15.—Section 6 of the Civil Liability Act 1961 is amended by—

(*a*) the deletion, in paragraph (*a*), of "or" where it last occurs, and

(*b*) the insertion of the following paragraph: 5

"(*a*a) a cause of action for violation of privacy within the meaning of the *Privacy Act 2006*, or".

Saver.

16.—This Act shall not affect causes of action accruing before its commencement.

Short title and commencement.

17.—(1) This Act may be cited as the Privacy Act 2006.

(2) This Act shall come into operation one month after the date of its passing.

AN BILLE UM PRÍOBHÁIDEACHT 2006

PRIVACY BILL 2006

EXPLANATORY AND FINANCIAL MEMORANDUM

Purpose of the Bill

1. The purpose of the Bill is to provide for a new tort of violation of privacy taking into account the jurisprudence of our courts and the European Court of Human Rights.

Definitions

2. *Section 1* is a standard provision defining certain terms used in the Bill.

Tort of violation of privacy

3. *Section 2* provides that it is a tort for a person wilfully and without lawful authority to violate the privacy of an individual. The tort is actionable without proof of special damage.

Entitlement to privacy

4. *Section 3* provides that a person's entitlement to privacy is that which might be reasonable in all the circumstances having regard to the rights of others and to public order and the common good. Without prejudice to the generality of the entitlement, there shall be a violation of privacy, subject to the provisions of *sections 5* (defences) and *6* (certain disclosures

not a violation of privacy), by subjecting another person to surveillance and by the disclosure of information so obtained; by (unauthorised) use of name, voice or likeness of an individual for commercial purpose; by the disclosure of personal information or documents of a person or to commit an act (of harassment) as described in section 10 of the Non-Fatal Offences Against the Person Act 1997.

Matters to which the court shall have regard

5. *Section 4* provides for a range of factors to which a court shall have regard in determining whether a violation of privacy of an individual has occurred.

Defences

6. *Section 5* provides for a number of defences to an allegation of violation of privacy. These essentially involve where the act was that of a public servant acting or reasonably believing themselves to be acting in the course of their duties, the installation and operation of a closed circuit television system for a purpose authorised by law or for the protection of persons or property, for the prevention or investigation of crime or under the law or was an act of newsgathering by a newspaper or broadcaster provided that any disclosure of material obtained was done in good faith, was for the purpose of discussing a subject of public importance, was for the public benefit and was fair and reasonable in all of the circumstances.

Certain disclosures not a violation of privacy

7. *Section 6* provides for a number of instances whereby the disclosure of any matter concerning an individual is not a violation of privacy. These include where the disclosure was done in good faith for the purpose of discussing a subject of public importance, in circumstances of privilege, by a public servant in the course of their duties and as provided for under the Data Processing Acts.

Jurisdiction of courts

8. *Section 7* provides a jurisdiction for actions taken in the Circuit Court where the claim does not exceed €50,000.

Remedies

9. *Section 8* provides that in a privacy action the court may grant any one or more of the following remedies to the plaintiff: — an injunction, — award damages, — order the defendant to account to the plaintiff for profits that have accrued or may later accrue to the defendant because of

the violation of privacy, — order the defendant to deliver to the plaintiff any material, articles, photographs or documents that have come into the defendant's possession because of the violation of privacy, or — grant any other relief to the plaintiff that appears to the court proper in the circumstances.

Dismissal for want of prosecution

10. *Section 9* provides that in a privacy action in which no proceeding, required by rules of court, has been taken by the plaintiff during the period of one year from the beginning of the action, the action may be dismissed on application to the court by the defendant.

Appeals in privacy actions

11. *Section 10* is self explanatory.

Limitation of action

12. *Section 11* provides that a privacy action must be brought within a period of one year from the discovery of the alleged acts, though a court may extend this period to 2 years.

Notice of intention to bring action

13. *Section 12* is self explanatory.

Hearing of action other than in public

14. *Section 13* provides that a court may on the application of a person who claims that his or her rights under the Act have been or are about to be infringed, hear any or all of an action for violation of privacy other than in public.

Trial of Privacy Action

15. *Section 14* provides that a privacy action shall be tried without a jury.

Extinguishment of cause of action on death

16. *Section 15* provides that a right of action for violation of privacy is extinguished on the death of the person alleging the infringement.

Saver

17. *Section 16* provides that the Act should only apply to a cause of

action which accrues after it comes into operation.

Short title and Commencement

18. *Section 17* is a standard provision and proposes that the Act shall come into operation one month after its passing.

Financial Implications

19. There are no discernable financial implications for the Exchequer.

APPENDIX 7

AN BILLE UM CHLÚMHILLEADH 2006

DEFAMATION BILL 2006

Mar a tionscnaíodh
As initiated

ARRANGEMENT OF SECTIONS

PART 1
PRELIMINARY AND GENERAL

PART 2
DEFAMATION

PART 3
DEFENCES

20. Offer to make amends.
21. Effect of offer to make amends.
22. Apology.
23. Consent to publish.
24. Fair and reasonable publication on a matter of public importance.
25. Innocent publication.

PART 4

REMEDIES

26. Declaratory order.
27. Lodgment of money in settlement of action.
28. Correction order.
29. Damages.
30. Aggravated and punitive damages.
31. Dismissal for want of prosecution.
32. Order prohibiting the publication of a defamatory statement.
33. Summary disposal of action.

PART 5

CRIMINAL LIABILITY

34. Abolition of certain common law offences.
35. Publication of gravely harmful statements.
36. Seizure of copies of false statements.

PART 6

MISCELLANEOUS

37. Limitation of actions.
38. Survival of cause of action on death.
39. Agreements for indemnity.
40. Jurisdiction of courts.
41. Malicious falsehood.
42. Evidence of acquittal or conviction.
43. Press Council.

SCHEDULE 1

STATEMENTS HAVING QUALIFIED PRIVILEGE

PART 1

STATEMENTS PRIVILEGED WITHOUT EXPLANATION OR CONTRADICTION

PART 2
STATEMENTS PRIVILEGED SUBJECT TO EXPLANATION OR CONTRADICTION

SCHEDULE 2
MINIMUM REQUIREMENTS IN RELATION TO PRESS COUNCIL

ACTS REFERRED TO

Arbitration (International Commercial) Act 1998	1998, No. 14
Arbitration Act 1954	1954, No. 26
Arbitration Act 1980	1980, No. 7
Civil Liability Act 1961	1961, No. 41
Commissions of Investigation Act 2004	2004, No. 23
Committees of the Houses of the Oireachtas (Privilege and Procedure) Act 1976	1976, No. 10
Courts (Supplemental Provisions) Act 1961	1961, No. 39
Courts Act 1991	1991, No. 20
Courts of Justice Act 1924	1924, No. 10
Defamation Act 1961	1961, No. 40
Irish Takeover Panel Act 1997	1997, No. 5
Statute of Limitations 1957	1957, No. 6
Tribunals of Inquiry (Evidence) Acts 1921 to 2004	

AN BILLE UM CHLÚMHILLEADH 2006

DEFAMATION BILL 20066

BILL

entitled

AN ACT TO REVISE IN PART THE LAW OF DEFAMATION; TO REPEAL THE DEFAMATION ACT 1961; AND TO PROVIDE FOR MATTERS CONNECTED THEREWITH.

BE IT ENACTED BY THE OIREACHTAS AS FOLLOWS:

PART 1
PRELIMINARY AND GENERAL

Short title and commencement.

1.—(1) This Act may be cited as the Defamation Act 2006.

(2) This Act shall come into operation on such day or days as the Minister may appoint, by order or orders, either generally or with reference to any particular purpose or provision, and different days may be so appointed for different purposes and different provisions.

Definitions.

2.—In this Act—

"Act of 1957" means the Statute of Limitations 1957;

"Act of 1961" means the Defamation Act 1961;

"cause of action" means a cause of action for defamation;

"correction order" has the meaning assigned to it by *section 28*; 20

"declaratory order" has the meaning assigned to it by *section 26*;

"defamation" shall be construed in accordance with *section 5(2)*;

"defamation action" means—

(*a*) an action for damages for defamation, or

(*b*) an application for a declaratory order,

whether or not a claim for other relief under this Act is made;

"defamatory statement" means a statement that tends to injure a person's reputation in the eyes of reasonable members of society, and "defamatory" shall be construed accordingly;

"defence of absolute privilege" has the meaning assigned to it by *section 15*;

"defence of qualified privilege" has the meaning assigned to it by *section 16*;

"defence of truth" has the meaning assigned to it by *section 14*;

"electronic communication" includes a communication of information in the form of data, text, images or sound (or any combination of these) by means of guided or unguided electromagnetic energy, or both;

"Minister" means the Minister for Justice, Equality and Law Reform;

"periodical" means any newspaper, magazine, journal or other publication that is printed, published or issued, or that circulates, in the State at regular or substantially regular intervals and includes any version thereof published on the internet or by other electronic means;

"plaintiff" includes a defendant counterclaiming in respect of a statement that is alleged to be defamatory;

"Press Council" has the meaning assigned to it by *section 43*;

"Press Ombudsman" has the meaning assigned to it by *paragraph 8* of *Schedule 2*;

"qualified offer" has the meaning assigned to it by *section 20*;

"special damages" has the meaning assigned to it by *section 29(7)*;

"statement" includes—

(*a*) a statement made orally or in writing,

(*b*) visual images, sounds, gestures and any other method of signifying meaning,

(*c*) a statement—

(i) broadcast on the radio or television, or

(ii) published on the internet, and

(*d*) an electronic communication;

"summary relief" means, in relation to a defamation action—

(*a*) a correction order, or 35

(*b*) an order prohibiting further publication of the statement to which the action relates.

Saver.

3.—(1) A provision of this Act shall not affect causes of action accruing before its commencement.

(2) A provision of this Act shall not affect the operation of the general law in relation to defamation, in force immediately before its commencement, except to the extent that that provision provides otherwise (whether expressly or by necessary implication).

Repeal.

4.—The Act of 1961 is repealed.

PART 2

DEFAMATION

Defamation.

5.—(1) The tort of libel and the tort of slander—

(*a*) shall cease to be so described, and

(*b*) shall, instead, be collectively described, and are referred to in this Act, as the "tort of defamation".

(2) The tort of defamation consists of the publication, by any means, of a defamatory statement concerning a person to one or more than one person (other than the first-mentioned person), and "defamation" shall be construed accordingly.

(3) A defamatory statement concerns a person if it could reasonably be understood as referring to him or her.

(4) There shall be no publication for the purposes of the tort of defamation if the defamatory statement concerned is published to the person to whom it relates and to a person other than the person to whom it relates in circumstances where—

(*a*) it was not intended that the statement would be published to the second-mentioned person, and (*b*) it was not reasonably foreseeable that publication of the statement to the first-mentioned person would result in its being published to the second-mentioned person.

(5) The tort of defamation is actionable without proof of special damage.

Amendment of certain enactments.

6.—(1) Section 77 of the Courts of Justice Act 1924 is amended, in paragraph (i) (inserted by section 4(a) of the Courts Act 1991), by the substitution of "the tort of defamation" for the words "slander, libel".

(2) The Civil Liability Act 1961 is amended—

(*a*) in section 11, by—

(i) the substitution, in subsection (5), of "defamatory statement" for the words "libel or slander", and

(ii) the insertion of the following subsection:

"(7) In this section 'defamatory statement' has the same meaning as it has in the *Defamation Act 2006*.", and

(*b*) in section 14(6), by the substitution of "a defamation action under the *Defamation Act 2006*" for the words "an action for libel or slander".

Verifying affidavit.

7.—(1) Where the plaintiff in a defamation action—

(*a*) serves on the defendant any pleading containing assertions or allegations of fact, or

(*b*) provides further information to the defendant,

the plaintiff (or in the case of a defamation action brought on behalf of an infant or person of unsound mind by a next friend or a committee of the infant or person, the next friend or committee) shall swear an affidavit verifying those assertions or allegations, or that further information.

(2) Where the defendant in a defamation action—

(*a*) serves on the plaintiff any pleading containing assertions or allegations of fact, or

(*b*) provides further information to the plaintiff,

the defendant shall swear an affidavit verifying those assertions or allegations, or that further information.

(3) Where a defamation action is brought on behalf of an infant or a person of unsound mind by a next friend or a committee of the infant or person, an affidavit to which *subsection (1)* applies sworn by the next friend or committee concerned shall, in respect of assertions, allegations or further information, of which he or she does not have personal knowledge, state that he or she honestly believes the assertions, allegations or further information, to be true.

(4) Where the plaintiff or defendant in a defamation action is a body corporate, the person swearing the affidavit on behalf of the body corporate under *subsection (1)* or *(2)*, as the case may be, shall, in respect of assertions, allegations or further information, of which he or she does not have personal knowledge, state that he or she honestly believes the assertions, allegations or further information to be true.

(5) An affidavit under this section shall be sworn and filed in court not later than 2 months after the service of the pleading concerned or the provision of the further information concerned, as the case may be, or such longer period as the court may direct or the parties may agree.

(6) If a person makes a statement in an affidavit under this section—

(*a*) that is false or misleading in any material respect, and

(*b*) that he or she knows to be false or misleading,

he or she shall be guilty of an offence.

(7) A person guilty of an offence under this section shall be liable—

(*a*) on summary conviction, to a fine not exceeding €3,000, or imprisonment for a term not exceeding 6 months or to both, or

(*b*) on conviction on indictment, to a fine not exceeding €50,000, or imprisonment for a term not exceeding 5 years, or to both.

(8) An affidavit sworn under this section shall include a statement by the deponent that he or she is aware that the making of a statement by him or her in the affidavit that is false or misleading in any material respect and that he or she knows to be false or misleading is an offence.

(9) In a defamation action—

(*a*) the defendant shall, unless the court otherwise directs, be entitled to cross examine the plaintiff in relation to any statement made by the plaintiff in the affidavit sworn by him or her under this section, and

(*b*) the plaintiff shall, unless the court otherwise directs, be entitled to cross examine the defendant in relation to any statement made by the defendant in the affidavit sworn by him or her under this section.

(10) Where a plaintiff or a defendant fails to comply with this section, the court may make such order as it considers just and equitable, including—

(*a*) in the case of such a failure on the part of the plaintiff, an order dismissing the defamation action, and

(*b*) in the case of such a failure by the defendant, judgment in favour of the plaintiff,

and may give such directions in relation to an order so made as the court considers necessary or expedient.

(11) The reference to court in *subsection (5)* shall—

(*a*) in the case of a defamation action brought in the High Court, include a reference to the Master of the High

Court, and

(b) in the case of a defamation action brought in the Circuit Court, include a reference to the county registrar for the county in which the proceedings concerned were issued.

(12) (a) References in this section to plaintiff shall, in the case of a plaintiff who is deceased, be construed as references to his or her personal representative.

(b) References in this section to defendant shall, in the case of a defendant who is deceased, be construed as references to his or her personal representative.

(13) This section does not apply to an application for a declaratory order.

Imputation.

8.—A person has one cause of action only in respect of the publication of a defamatory statement concerning the person even if more than one defamatory imputation in respect of that person is borne by that statement.

Defamation of class of persons.

9.—Where a person publishes a defamatory statement concerning a class of persons, a member of that class shall have a cause of action under this Act against that person if—

(a) by reason of the number of persons who are members of that class, or

(b) by virtue of the circumstances in which the statement is published,

the statement could reasonably be understood to refer, in particular, to the member concerned.

Multiple publication.

10.—(1) Subject to *subsection (2)*, a person has one cause of action only in respect of a multiple publication.

(2) A court may grant leave to a person to bring more than one defamation action in respect of a multiple publication where it considers that the interests of justice so require.

(3) In this section "multiple publication" means publication by a person of the same defamatory statement to 2 or more persons (other than the person in respect of whom the statement is made) whether contemporaneously or not.

Defamation of a body corporate.

11.—The provisions of this Act apply to a body corporate as they apply to a natural person, and a body corporate may bring a defamation action under this Act in respect of a statement concerning it that it claims is defamatory whether or not it has incurred or is likely to incur financial loss as a result of the publication of that statement.

Appeals in defamation actions.

12.—(1) Upon the hearing of an appeal from a decision of the High Court in a defamation action, the Supreme Court may, in addition to any other order that it deems appropriate to make, substitute for any amount of damages awarded to the plaintiff by the High Court such amount as it considers appropriate.

(2) In this section "decision" includes a judgment entered pursuant to the verdict of a jury.

Meaning.

13.—(1) The court, in a defamation action, may give a ruling—

(*a*) as to whether the statement in respect of which the action was brought is reasonably capable of bearing the imputation pleaded by the plaintiff, and

(*b*) (where the court rules that that statement is reasonably capable of bearing that imputation) as to whether that imputation is reasonably capable of bearing a defamatory meaning,

upon an application being made to it in that behalf.

(2) Where a court rules under *subsection (1)* that—

(*a*) the statement in respect of which the action was brought is not reasonably capable of bearing the imputation pleaded by the plaintiff, or

(*b*) that any imputation so pleaded is not reasonably capable of bearing a defamatory meaning,

it shall dismiss the action in so far only as it relates to the imputation concerned.

(3) An application under this section shall be brought by notice of motion and shall be determined, in the case of a defamation action brought in the High Court, in the absence of the jury.

(4) An application under this section may be brought at any time after the bringing of the defamation action concerned including during the course of the trial of the action.

PART 3

DEFENCES

Truth.

14.—(1) It shall be a defence (to be known and in this Act referred to as the "the defence of truth") to a defamation action for the defendant to prove that the statement in respect of which the action was brought is true in all material respects.

(2) In a defamation action in respect of a statement containing 2 or more distinct allegations against the plaintiff, the defence of truth shall not fail by reason only of the truth of every allegation not being proved, if the words not proved to be true do not materially injure the plaintiff's reputation having regard to the truth of the remaining allegations.

Absolute privilege.

15.—(1) It shall be a defence to a defamation action for the defendant to prove that the statement in respect of which the action was brought would, if it had been made immediately before the commencement of this Act in accordance with *section 1(2)*, have been considered under the law in force immediately before such commencement as having been made on an occasion of absolute privilege.

(2) Without prejudice to the generality of *subsection (1)*, it shall be a defence to a defamation action for the defendant to prove that the statement in respect of which the action was brought was—

(*a*) made in either House of the Oireachtas by a member of either House of the Oireachtas,

(*b*) contained in a report of a statement, to which *paragraph (a)* applies, produced by or on the authority of either such House,

(*c*) made in the European Parliament by a member of that Parliament,

(*d*) contained in a report of a statement, to which *paragraph (c)* applies, produced by or on the authority of the European Parliament,

(*e*) contained in a judgment of a court established by law in the State,

(*f*) made by a judge, or other person, performing a judicial function,

(*g*) made by a party, witness, legal representative or juror in the course of proceedings presided over by a judge, or other person, performing a judicial function,

(*h*) made in the course of proceedings involving the exercise of limited functions and powers of a judicial nature in accordance with Article 37 of the Constitution, where the statement is connected with those proceedings,

(*i*) a fair and accurate report of proceedings publicly heard before, or decision made public by, any court—

(i) established by law in the State, or

(ii) established under the law of Northern Ireland,

(*j*) a fair and accurate report of proceedings publicly heard before, or decision made public by, any court or arbitral tribunal established by an international agreement to which the State is a party including the Court of Justice of the European Communities, the Court of First Instance of the European Communities, the European Court of Human Rights and the International Court of Justice,

(*k*) made in proceedings before a committee of either House of the Oireachtas,

(*l*) made in proceedings before a committee of the European Parliament,

(*m*) made in the course of proceedings before a tribunal established under the Tribunals of Inquiry (Evidence) Acts 1921 to 2004, where the statement is connected with those proceedings,

(*n*) contained in a report of any such tribunal,

(*o*) made in the course of proceedings before a commission of investigation established under the Commissions of Investigation Act 2004, where the statement is connected with those proceedings,

(*p*) contained in a report of any such commission,

(*q*) made in the course of an inquest by a coroner or contained in a decision made or verdict given at or during such inquest,

(*r*) made in the course of an inquiry conducted on the authority of a Minister of the Government, the Government, the Oireachtas, either House of the Oireachtas or a court established under the Constitution,

(*s*) made in the course of an inquiry conducted in Northern Ireland on the authority of a person or body corresponding to a person or body referred to in *paragraph (r)*,

(*t*) contained in a report of an inquiry referred to in *paragraph (r)* or *(s)*,

(*u*) made pursuant to and in accordance with an order of a court established by law in the State.

(3) Section 2 of the Committees of the Houses of the Oireachtas (Privilege and Procedure) Act 1976 is amended by the insertion of the following subsection:

"(3) In this section 'utterance' includes a statement within the meaning of the *Defamation Act 2006*;".

(4) Section 12 of the Arbitration (International Commercial) Act 1998 shall apply in relation to proceedings before an arbitral tribunal to which the Arbitration Act 1954 or the Arbitration Act 1980 applies.

(5) A defence under this section shall be known as, and is referred to in this Act, as the "defence of absolute privilege".

Qualified privilege.

16.—(1) Subject to *section 15*, it shall be a defence to a defamation action for the defendant to prove that the statement in respect of which the action was brought would, if it had been made immediately before the commencement of this Act in accordance with *section 1(2)*, have been considered under the law (other than the Act of 1961) in force immediately before such commencement as having been made on an occasion of qualified privilege.

(2) Without prejudice to the generality of *subsection (1)*, it shall, subject to *section 17*, be a defence to a defamation action for the defendant to prove that—

- (*a*) the statement was published to a person or persons who—
  - (i) had a duty to receive, or interest in receiving, the information contained in the statement, or
  - (ii) the defendant believed upon reasonable grounds that the said person or persons had such a duty or interest, and
- (*b*) the defendant had a corresponding duty to communicate, or interest in communicating, the information to such person or persons.

(3) Without prejudice to the generality of *subsection (1)* it shall, subject to *section 17*, be a defence to a defamation action for the defendant to prove that the statement to which the action relates is contained in a report specified in *Schedule* 1, unless in the case of a report or other matter referred to in *Part 2* of that *Schedule*,it is proved that the defendant was requested by the plaintiff to publish in the same medium of communication in which he or she published the statement concerned, a reasonable statement by way of explanation or a contradiction, and has refused or failed to do so or has done so in a manner that is not adequate or reasonable having regard to all the circumstances.

(4) Nothing in *subsection (3)* shall be construed as—

- (*a*) protecting the publication of any statement the publication of which is prohibited by law, or of any statement that is not of public concern and the publication of which is not for the public benefit, or
- (*b*) limiting or abridging any privilege subsisting apart from *subsection (3)*.

(5) A defence under this section shall be known, and is referred to in this Act, as the "defence of qualified privilege".

(6) In this section—

"duty" means a legal, moral or social duty.

"interest" means a legal, moral or social interest.

Loss of defence of qualified privilege.

17.—(1) In a defamation action, the defence of qualified privilege shall fail if, in relation to the publication of the statement in respect of which the action was brought, the plaintiff proves that—

(*a*) the defendant did not believe the statement to be true,

(*b*) the defendant acted in bad faith or out of spite, ill will or improper motive,

(*c*) the statement bore no relation to the purpose of the defence, or

(*d*) the manner and extent of publication of the statement exceeded what was reasonably sufficient in all the circumstances.

(2) The defence of qualified privilege shall not fail by reason only of the publication of the statement concerned to a person other than an interested person if it is proved that the statement was published to the person because the publisher mistook him or her for an interested person.

(3) Where a defamation action is brought against more than one defendant, the failure of the defence of qualified privilege in relation to one of the defendants by virtue of the application of *subsection (1)* shall not cause the failure of the defence in relation to another of the defendants unless that other defendant was vicariously liable for such acts or omissions of the first-mentioned defendant as gave rise to the cause of action concerned.

(4) Section 11(4) of the Civil Liability Act 1961 is repealed.

(5) In this section "interested person" means, in relation to a statement, a person who, under *section 16(2)(a)*, had a duty or interest in receiving the information contained in the statement.

Honest opinion.

18.—(1) It shall be a defence (to be known, and in this Act referred to, as the "defence of honest opinion") to a defamation action for the defendant to prove that, in the case of a statement consisting of an opinion, the opinion was honestly held.

(2) Subject to *subsection (3)*, an opinion is honestly held, for the purposes of this section, if—

(*a*) at the time of the publication of the statement, the defendant believed in the truth of the opinion or, where the defendant is not the author of the opinion, believed that the author believed it to be true,

(b) (i) the opinion was based on allegations of fact—

(I) specified in the statement containing the opinion, or

(II) referred to in that statement, that were known, or might reasonably be expected to have been known, by the persons to whom the statement was published,

or

(ii) the opinion was based on allegations of fact to which—

(I) the defence of absolute privilege, or

(II) the defence of qualified privilege in accordance with *section 16(2)*,

would apply if a defamation action were brought in respect of such allegations,

and

(c) the opinion related to a matter of public importance.

(3) (a) Where a defendant pleads the defence of honest opinion and the opinion concerned is based on allegations of fact to which *subsection (2)(b)(i)* applies, that defence shall fail unless the defendant proves the truth of those allegations, but the defence shall not fail by reason only of the defendant's failing to prove the truth of all of those allegations if the opinion is honest opinion having regard to the allegations of fact the truth of which is proved.

(b) Where a defendant pleads the defence of honest opinion and the opinion concerned is based on allegations of fact to which *subsection (2)(b)(ii)* applies, that defence shall not fail by reason only of the defendant's failing to prove the truth of those allegations unless—

(i) the opinion could reasonably be understood as implying that those allegations are true, or

(ii) the allegations are untrue and, at the time of the publication of the opinion, the defendant knew or ought reasonably to have known that those allegations were untrue.

(4) Where a defamatory statement consisting of an opinion is published jointly by a person ("first-mentioned person") and another person ("joint publisher"), the first-mentioned person shall not fail in pleading the defence of honest opinion in a subsequent defamation action brought in respect of that statement by reason only of that opinion not being honestly held by the joint publisher, unless the first-mentioned person was at the time of

publication vicariously liable for the acts or omissions, from which the cause of action in respect of that statement accrued, of the joint publisher.

Distinguishing between allegations of fact and opinion.

19.—The matters to which the court in a defamation action shall have regard, for the purposes of distinguishing between a statement consisting of allegations of fact and a statement consisting of opinion, shall include the following:

(*a*) the extent to which the statement is capable of being proved;

(*b*) the extent to which the statement was made in circumstances in which it was likely to have been reasonably understood as a statement of opinion rather than a statement consisting of an allegation of fact; and

(*c*) the words used in the statement and the extent to which the statement was subject to a qualification or a disclaimer or was accompanied by cautionary words.

Offer to make amends.

20.—(1) A person who has published a statement that is alleged to be defamatory of another person may make an offer to make amends.

(2) An offer to make amends shall—

(*a*) be in writing,

(*b*) state that it is an offer to make amends for the purposes of this section, and

(*c*) state whether the offer is in respect of the entire of the statement or an offer (in this Act referred to as a "qualified offer") in respect of—

(i) part only of the statement, or

(ii) a particular defamatory meaning only.

(3) An offer to make amends shall not be made after the delivery of the defence in the defamation action concerned.

(4) An offer to make amends may be withdrawn before it is accepted and where such an offer is withdrawn a new offer to make amends may be made.

(5) In this section "an offer to make amends" means an offer—

(*a*) to make a suitable correction of the statement concerned and a sufficient apology to the person to whom the statement refers or is alleged to refer,

(*b*) to publish that correction and apology in such manner as is reasonable and practicable in the circumstances, and (*c*) to pay to the person such sum in compensation or damages (if any), and such costs, as may be agreed by them or as may be determined to be payable,

whether or not it is accompanied by any other offer to perform an act other than an act referred to in *paragraph (a)*, *(b)* or *(c)*.

Effect of offer to make amends.

21.—(1) If an offer to make amends under *section 20* is accepted the following provisions shall apply:

(*a*) if the parties agree as to the measures that should be taken by the person who made the offer to ensure compliance by him or her with the terms of the offer, the High Court or, where a defamation action has already been brought, the court in which it was brought may, upon the application of the person to whom the offer was made, direct the party who made the offer to take those measures;

(*b*) if the parties do not so agree, the person who made the offer may, with the leave of the High Court or, where a defamation action has already been brought, the court in which it was brought, make a correction and apology by means of a statement before the court in such terms as may be approved by the court and give an undertaking as to the manner of their publication;

(*c*) if the parties do not agree as to the damages or costs that should be paid by the person who made the offer, those matters shall be determined by the High Court or, where a defamation action has already been brought, the court in which it was brought, and the court shall for those purposes have all such powers as it would have if it were determining damages or costs in a defamation action, and in making a determination under this paragraph it shall take into account the adequacy of any measures already taken to ensure compliance with the terms of the offer by the person who made the offer;

(*d*) no defamation action shall be brought or, if already brought, proceeded with against another person in respect of the statement to which the offer to make amends applies unless the court considers that in all the circumstances of the case it is just and proper to so do.

(2) Subject to *subsection (3)*, it shall be a defence to a defamation action for a person to prove that he or she made an offer to make amends under

section 20 and that it was not accepted, unless the plaintiff proves that the defendant knew or ought reasonably to have known at the time of making the statement to which the offer relates that—

(*a*) it referred to the plaintiff or was likely to be understood as referring to the plaintiff, and

(*b*) it was false and defamatory of the plaintiff.

(3) Where the defendant in a defamation action made a qualified offer only, *subsection (2)* shall apply in relation to that part only of the action that relates to the part of the statement or the meaning, as the case may be, to which the qualified offer relates.

(4) A person who makes an offer to make amends is not required to plead it as a defence in a defamation action.

(5) If a defendant in a defamation action pleads the defence under this section, he or she shall not be entitled to plead any other defence in the action, and if the defence is pleaded in respect of a qualified offer only he or she shall not be entitled to plead any other defence in respect of that part of the action that relates to the part of the statement or the meaning, as the case may be, to which the qualified offer relates.

Apology.

22.—(1) In a defamation action the defendant may give evidence, in mitigation of damage, that he or she made or offered an apology to the plaintiff in respect of the statement to which the action relates, either—

(*a*) before the bringing of the action, or

(*b*) as soon as practicable thereafter, in circumstances where the action was commenced before there was an opportunity to make or offer an apology.

(2) In a defamation action, a defendant who intends to give evidence to which *subsection (1)* applies shall, at the time of the filing or delivery of the defence to the action, notify the plaintiff in writing of his or her intention to give such evidence.

(3) In a defamation action, an apology made by or on behalf of a defendant in respect of a statement to which the action relates—

(*a*) does not constitute an express or implied admission of liability by that defendant, and

(*b*) is not relevant to the determination of liability in the action.

(4) Evidence of an apology made by or on behalf of a person in respect of a statement to which the action relates is not admissible in any civil proceedings as evidence of liability of the defendant.

Consent to publish.

23.—In a defamation action it shall be a defence, to be known as the "defence of consent", for a person to prove that the plaintiff consented to the publication of the statement in respect of which the action was brought.

Fair and reasonable publication on a matter of public importance.

24.—(1) Subject to *subsection (4)*, it shall be a defence (to be known, and in this section referred to, as "the defence of fair and reasonable publication") to a defamation action for the defendant to prove that the statement in respect of which the action was brought was published—

(*a*) in good faith, and

(*b*) in the course of, or for the purposes of, the discussion of a subject of public importance, the discussion of which was for the public benefit,

and in all the circumstances of the case, it was fair and reasonable to publish the statement.

(2) For the purposes of this section, the court shall, in determining whether it was fair and reasonable to publish the statement concerned, take into account such matters as the court considers relevant including any or all of the following:

(*a*) the extent to which the statement concerned refers to the performance by the person of his or her public functions;

(*b*) the seriousness of any allegations made in the statement;

(*c*) the context and content (including the language used) of the statement;

(*d*) the extent to which the statement drew a distinction between suspicions, allegations and facts;

(*e*) the extent to which there were exceptional circumstances that necessitated the publication of the statement on the date of publication;

(*f*) in the case of a statement published in a periodical, the extent to which the publisher of the periodical—

(i) adhered to the code of standards of the Press Council or to standards equivalent to those specified in that code of standards, and

(ii) abided by decisions of the Press Ombudsman and determinations of the Press Council;

(*g*) the extent to which the plaintiff's version of events was represented in the publication concerned and, if not so represented, the extent to which a reasonable attempt was made by the publisher to obtain and publish a response from that person;

(*h*) any other means taken to verify the assertions and allegations concerning the plaintiff in the statement.

(3) The failure or refusal of a plaintiff to respond to attempts by or on behalf of the defendant, to elicit the plaintiff's version of events, shall not—

(*a*) constitute or imply consent to the publication of the statement, or

(*b*) entitle the court to draw an inference if, in the particular circumstances of the case, the court considers that the plaintiff was reasonable in withholding any response or in believing that a denial or refutation by the plaintiff of a defamatory statement would itself be unfairly used or published.

(4) The defence of fair and reasonable publication shall fail unless, in relation to the publication of the statement in respect of which the action was brought, the defendant proves that—

(*a*) at the time of publication he or she believed the statement to be true,

(*b*) he or she did not act in bad faith or out of spite, ill will or other improper motive,

(*c*) the statement bore a relation to the purpose of the defence, and

(*d*) the manner and extent of publication of the statement did not exceed that which was reasonably sufficient in all of the circumstances.

(5) In this section—

"court" means, in relation to a defamation action brought in the High Court, the jury, if the High Court is sitting with a jury;

"defamation action" does not include an application for a declaratory order.

Innocent publication.

25.—(1) It shall be a defence (to be known as the "defence of innocent publication") to a defamation action for the defendant to prove that—

(*a*) he or she was not the author, editor or publisher of the statement to which the action relates,

(*b*) he or she took reasonable care in relation to its publication, and

(*c*) he or she did not know, and had no reason to believe, that what he or she did caused or contributed to the publication of a statement that would give rise to a cause of action in defamation.

(2) A person shall not, for the purposes of this section, be considered to be the author, editor or publisher of a statement if—

(*a*) in relation to printed material containing the statement, he or she was responsible for the printing, production, distribution or selling only of the printed material, (*b*) in relation to a film or sound recording containing the statement, he or she was responsible for the processing, copying, distribution, exhibition or selling only of the film or sound recording,

(*c*) in relation to any electronic medium on which the statement is recorded or stored, he or she was responsible for the processing, copying, distribution or selling only of the electronic medium or was responsible for the operation or provision only of any equipment, system or service by means of which the statement would be capable of being retrieved, copied, distributed or made available.

(3) The court shall, for the purposes of determining whether a person took reasonable care, or had reason to believe that what he or she did caused or contributed to the publication of a defamatory statement, have regard to—

(*a*) the extent of the person's responsibility for the content of the statement or the decision to publish it,

(*b*) the nature or circumstances of the publication, and

(*c*) the previous conduct or character of the person.

PART 4
Remedies

Declaratory order.

26.—(1) A person who claims to be the subject of a statement that he or she alleges is defamatory may apply to the High Court for an order (in this Act referred to as a "declaratory order") that the statement is false and defamatory of him or her.

(2) Upon an application under this section, the court shall make a declaratory order if it is satisfied that—

(*a*) the statement is defamatory of the applicant and the respondent has no defence to the application,

(*b*) the applicant requested the respondent to make an apology, correction or retraction in relation to that statement, and

(*c*) the respondent failed or refused to accede to that request.

(3) Where an application is made under this section, the applicant shall not be entitled to bring any other proceedings in respect of any cause of action arising out of the statement to which the application relates.

(4) An application under this section shall be heard by a judge sitting alone.

(5) An application under this section shall be brought by motion on

notice to the respondent grounded on affidavit.

(6) Where a court makes a declaratory order, it may, in addition, make an order under *section 28* or *32*, upon an application by the applicant in that behalf.

(7) The court may, for the purposes of making a determination in relation to an application under this section in an expeditious manner, give directions in relation to the delivery of pleadings and the time and manner of trial of any issues raised in the course of such an application.

(8) No order in relation to damages shall be made upon an application under this section.

Lodgment of money in settlement of action.

27.—(1) In an action for damages for defamation the defendant may, upon giving notice in writing to the plaintiff, pay a sum of money into court in satisfaction of the action when filing his or her defence to the action.

(2) A payment to which this section applies shall be deemed to be a payment under such rule of court for the time being in force as provides for the payment into court of a sum of money in satisfaction of an action for damages for defamation.

(3) Where a payment to which this section applies is made, the plaintiff in the action concerned may accept the payment—

(*a*) in accordance with the rule referred to in *subsection (2)*,or

(*b*) inform the court in which the action was brought, on notice to the defendant, of his or her acceptance of the payment in full settlement of the action.

(4) The defendant shall not be required to admit liability in an action for damages for defamation when making a payment to which this section applies.

Correction order.

28.—(1) Where, in a defamation action, there is a finding that the statement in respect of which the action was brought was defamatory and the defendant has no defence to the action, the court may, upon the application of the plaintiff, make an order (in this Act referred to as a "correction order") directing the defendant to publish a correction of the defamatory statement.

(2) Without prejudice to the generality of *subsection (1)*, a correction order shall specify—

(*a*) the date and time upon which the correction shall be published, and

(*b*) the form, content, extent and manner of publication of the correction, and shall, unless the plaintiff otherwise requests, require the correction to be published in such manner as will ensure that it is communicated to all or substantially all of those persons to whom the defamatory statement was published.

(3) Where a plaintiff in a defamation action intends to make an application under this section, he or she shall—

(*a*) so inform the defendant, by notice in writing, not later than 7 days before the trial of the action, and

(*b*) at the trial of the action, so inform the court.

(4) An application under this section may be made at such time during the trial of a defamation action as the court or, where the action is tried in the High Court sitting with a jury, the trial judge directs.

Damages.

29.—(1) The parties in a defamation action may make submissions to the court in relation to the matter of damages.

(2) In a defamation action brought in the High Court, the judge shall give directions to the jury in relation to the matter of damages.

(3) In making an award of general damages in a defamation action, regard shall be had to all of the circumstances of the case.

(4) Without prejudice to the generality of *subsection (3)*, the court in a defamation action shall, in making an award of general damages, have regard to—

(*a*) the nature and gravity of any allegation in the defamatory statement concerned,

(*b*) the means of publication of the defamatory statement including the enduring nature of those means,

(*c*) the extent to which the defamatory statement was circulated,

(*d*) the offering or making of any apology, correction or retraction by the defendant to the plaintiff in respect of the defamatory statement,

(*e*) the making of any offer to make amends under *section 20* by the defendant, whether or not the making of that offer was pleaded as a defence,

(*f*) the importance to the plaintiff of his or her reputation in the eyes of particular or all recipients of the defamatory statement,

(*g*) the extent (if at all) to which the plaintiff caused or contributed to, or acquiesced in, the publication of the defamatory statement,

(*h*) evidence given concerning the reputation of the plaintiff,

(*i*) if the defence of truth is pleaded and the defendant

proves the truth of part but not the whole of the defamatory statement, the extent to which that defence is successfully pleaded in relation to the statement,

(*j*) if the defence of qualified privilege is pleaded in accordance with *section 16(2)*, the extent to which the defendant has acceded to the request of the plaintiff to publish a reasonable statement by way of explanation or contradiction, and

(*k*) any order made under *section 32*, or any order under that section or correction order that the court proposes to make or, where the action is tried by the High Court sitting with a jury, would propose to make in the event of there being a finding of defamation.

(5) For the purposes of *subsection (4)(c)*, a defamatory statement consisting of words that are innocent on their face, but that are defamatory by reason of facts known to some recipients only of the publication containing the defamatory statement, shall be treated as having been published to those recipients only.

(6) The defendant in a defamation action may for the purposes of mitigating damages—

(*a*) give evidence of any matter that would have a bearing upon the reputation of the plaintiff, provided that it relates to matters connected with the defamatory statement,

(*b*) give evidence that the plaintiff has already in another defamation action been awarded damages in respect of a defamatory statement that contained substantially the same allegations as are contained in the defamatory statement to which the first-mentioned defamation action relates.

(7) The court in a defamation action may make an award of damages (in this section referred to as "special damages") to the plaintiff in respect of financial loss suffered by him or her as a result of the injury to his or her reputation caused by the publication of the defamatory statement in respect of which the action was brought.

(8) In this section "court" means, in relation to a defamation action brought in the High Court, the jury, if the High Court is sitting with a jury.

Aggravated and punitive damages.

30. —(1) Where, in a defamation action—

(*a*) the court finds the defendant liable to pay damages to the plaintiff in respect of a defamatory statement, and

(*b*) the defendant conducted his or her defence in a manner that aggravated the injury caused to the plaintiff's reputation by the defamatory statement,

the court may, in addition to any general, special or punitive damages payable by the defendant to the plaintiff, order the defendant to pay to the plaintiff damages (in this section referred to as "aggravated damages") of such amount as it considers appropriate to compensate the plaintiff for the aggravation of the said injury.

(2) Where, in a defamation action, the court finds the defendant liable to pay damages to the plaintiff in respect of a defamatory statement and it is proved that the defendant—

(*a*) intended to publish the defamatory statement concerned to a person other than the plaintiff,

(*b*) knew that the defamatory statement would be understood by the said person to refer to the plaintiff, and

(*c*) knew that the statement was untrue or in publishing it was reckless as to whether it was true or untrue,

the court may, in addition to any general, special or aggravated damages payable by the defendant to the plaintiff, order the defendant to pay to the plaintiff damages (in this section referred to as "punitive damages") of such amount as it considers appropriate.

(3) In this section "court" means, in relation to a defamation action brought in the High Court, the jury, if the High Court is sitting with a jury.

Dismissal for want of prosecution.

31.—(1) Where rules of court provide that the plaintiff in a defamation action is, not later than one year from the bringing of the defamation action, required to do any thing and the plaintiff fails to so do, the defendant may, upon the expiration of that period, apply to the court to have the action dismissed, and the court shall dismiss the action upon such application unless the dismissal of the action would result in injustice being done.

(2) An application under this section shall be brought by motion on notice to the plaintiff.

Order prohibiting the publication of a defamatory statement.

32.—(1) The High Court, or where a defamation action has been brought, the court in which it was brought, may, upon the application of the plaintiff, make an order prohibiting the publication or further publication of the statement in respect of which the application was made if in its opinion—

(*a*) the statement is defamatory, and

(*b*) the defendant has no defence to the action that is

reasonably likely to succeed.

(2) Where an order is made under this section it shall not operate to prohibit the reporting of the making of that order provided that such reporting does not include the publication of the statement to which the order relates.

(3) In this section "order" means—

(*a*) an interim order,

(*b*) an interlocutory order, or

(*c*) a permanent order.

Summary disposal of action.

33.—(1) The court in a defamation action may, upon the application of the plaintiff, grant summary relief to the plaintiff if it is satisfied that—

(*a*) the statement in respect of which the action was brought is defamatory, and

(*b*) the defendant has no defence to the action that is reasonably likely to succeed.

(2) The court in a defamation action may, upon the application of the defendant, dismiss the action if it is satisfied that the statement in respect of which the action was brought is not reasonably capable of being found to have a defamatory meaning.

(3) An application under this section shall be brought by motion on notice to the other party to the action and shall be grounded on an affidavit.

(4) An application under this section shall not be heard or determined in the presence of a jury.

PART 5

CRIMINAL LIABILITY

Abolition of certain common law offences.

34.—The common law offences of criminal libel, seditious libel and obscene libel are abolished.

Publication of gravely harmful statements.

35.—(1) A person who knowingly, and with the intention of causing grave injury to the reputation of a person (other than a body corporate), publishes or causes to be published a statement containing false allegations concerning the second-mentioned person, thereby causing grave injury to the reputation of the second-mentioned person, shall be guilty of an offence.

(2) A person who is guilty of an offence under this section shall be liable on conviction on indictment to a fine not exceeding €50,000 or to imprisonment for a term not exceeding 5 years or to both.

(3) *Part 3* shall apply to proceedings for an offence under this section

as it applies to a defamation action, and accordingly references in that part to a defamation action shall be construed as references to proceedings for an offence under this section.

(4) Proceedings for an offence under this section shall not be brought unless, not later than one year after the alleged commission of the offence—

(*a*) the Director of Public Prosecutions gives his or her consent to the proceedings being brought, or

(*b*) the High Court makes an order permitting the bringing of the proceedings.

(5) The District Court may try summarily a person charged with an offence under this section if—

(*a*) the court is of opinion that the facts alleged constitute a minor offence fit to be tried summarily,

(*b*) the accused, on being informed by the court of his or her right to be tried with a jury, does not object to being tried summarily for the offence, and

(*c*) the Director of Public Prosecutions consents to the accused being tried summarily for the offence.

(6) Upon conviction of a person by the District Court of an offence under this section, the person shall be liable to a fine not exceeding €5,000 or to imprisonment for a term not exceeding 12 months or to both.

(7) Where a person is convicted of an offence under this section the court may order that the person—

(*a*) shall not publish any statement of such a nature as the court shall specify for such period as the court shall specify concerning the person who was the subject of the false statement to which the offence related,

(*b*) shall not communicate with the person referred to in *paragraph (a)* by any means for such period as the court shall specify, and

(*c*) shall, in such manner as the court may specify, publish or cause to be published a statement that the false statement to which the offence related was false and caused grave damage to the reputation of the person referred to in *paragraph (a)*.

Seizure of copies of false statements.

36.—(1) Where a person is convicted of an offence under *section* 35, the court may issue a warrant—

(*a*) authorising any member of the Garda Síochána to enter (if necessary by the use of reasonable force) at all reasonable times any premises (including a dwelling) at which he or she has reasonable grounds for believing that copies of the statement to which offence related are to be found, and to search those premises and seize and remove all copies of the statement found therein,

(*b*) directing the seizure and removal by any member of the Garda Síochána of all copies of the statement to which the offence related that are in the possession of any person,

(*c*) specifying the manner in which copies so seized and removed shall be detained and stored by the Garda Síochána.

(2) A member of the Garda Síochána may—

(*a*) enter and search any premises,

(*b*) seize, remove and detain any copy of a statement to which an offence under *section 35* relates found therein or in the possession of any person,

in accordance with a warrant under *subsection (1)*.

(3) Upon final judgement being given in proceedings for an offence under *section 35*, anything seized and removed under *subsection (2)* shall be disposed of in accordance with such directions as the court may give upon an application by a member of the Garda Síochána in that behalf.

PART 6

MISCELLANEOUS

Limitation of actions.

37.—(1) Section 11 of the Act of 1957 is amended—

(*a*) in subsection (2), by the substitution of the following paragraph for paragraph (*c*):

"(c) A defamation action within the meaning of the *Defamation Act 2006* shall not be brought after the expiration of—

(i) one year, or

(ii) such longer period as the court may direct not exceeding 2 years,

from the date on which the cause of action accrued.",

and

(*b*) the insertion of the following subsections:

"(3A) The court shall not give a direction under subsection (2)(c)(ii) (inserted by *section 37(1)(a)* of the *Defamation Act 2006*) unless it is satisfied that—

(*a*) the interests of justice require the giving of the direction,

(*b*) the prejudice that the plaintiff would suffer if the direction were not given would significantly outweigh the prejudice that the defendant would suffer if the direction were given,

and the court shall, in deciding whether to give such a direction, have regard to the reason for the failure to bring the action within the period specified in subparagraph (i) of the said subsection (2)(c) and the extent to which any evidence relevant to the matter is by virtue of the delay no longer capable of being adduced.

(3B) For the purposes of bringing a defamation action within the meaning of the *Defamation Act 2006*, the date of accrual of the cause of action shall be the date upon which the defamatory statement is first published and, where the statement is published through the medium of the internet, the date on which it is first capable of being viewed or listened to through that medium.".

(2) Section 49 of the Act of 1957 is amended by the substitution of the following subsection for subsection (3):

"(3) In the case of defamation actions within the meaning of the *Defamation Act 2006*, subsection (1) of this section shall have effect as if for the words 'six years' there were substituted the words 'one year or such longer period as the court may direct not exceeding two years.'.".

Survival of cause of action on death.

38.—(1) Section 6 of the Civil Liability Act 1961 is amended by the insertion of the following definitions:

" 'Act of 2006' means the *Defamation Act 2006*;

'aggravated damages' has the same meaning as it has in the *Act of 2006*;

'punitive damages' has the same meaning as it has in the *Act of 2006*.".

(2) Section 7 of the Civil Liability Act 1961 is amended by—

(*a*) the insertion of the following subsection:

"(1A) On the death of a person on or after the commencement of *section 38(2)(a)* of the *Act of 2006*, a cause of action for defamation vested in him immediately before his death shall survive for the benefit of his estate.", and

(*b*) the insertion of the following subsection:

"(2A) Where by virtue of subsection (1A) of this section, a cause of action for defamation survives for the benefit of the estate of a deceased person, the damages recoverable for the benefit of the estate of that person shall not include general damages, punitive damages or aggravated damages.".

(3) Section 8 of the Civil Liability Act 1961 is amended by—

(*a*) the insertion of the following subsection:

"(1A) On the death of a person on or after the commencement of *section 38(3)(a)* of the *Act of 2006* a cause of action subsisting against him shall survive against his estate.",

(*b*) by the insertion of the following subsection:

"(2A) Where by virtue of subsection (1A) of this section, a cause of action for defamation survives against the estate of a deceased person, the damages recoverable against the estate of that person shall not include general damages, punitive damages or aggravated damages.".

Agreements for indemnity.

39.—An agreement to indemnify any person against civil liability for defamation in respect of the publication of any statement shall be lawful unless at the time of the publication that person knows that the statement is defamatory, and does not reasonably believe that there is a defence to any action brought upon it that would succeed.

Jurisdiction of courts.

40.—The Third Schedule to the Courts (Supplemental Provisions) Act 1961 is amended by—

(*a*) the insertion, in column (2) at reference number 6, of "a defamation action within the meaning of the *Defamation Act 2006*," between "other than" and "an action", and

(*b*) the insertion of the following:

"

7A	A defamation action under the *Defamation Act 2006*.	Where the amount of the claim does not exceed €50,000.	At the election of the plaintiff— (*a*) the judge of the circuit where the tort is alleged to have been committed, or (*b*) the judge of the circuit where the defendant or one of the defendants resides or carries on business.

".

Malicious falsehood.

41.—(1) In an action for slander of title, slander of goods or other malicious falsehood, the plaintiff shall be required to prove that the statement upon which the action is founded—

(*a*) was untrue, 15

(*b*) was published maliciously, and

(*c*) referred to the plaintiff, his or her property or his or her office, profession, calling, trade or business.

(2) In an action for slander of title, slander of goods or other malicious falsehood, the plaintiff shall be required to prove—

(*a*) special damage, or

(*b*) that the publication of the statement was calculated to cause and was likely to cause financial loss to the plaintiff in respect of his or her property or his or her office, profession, calling, trade or business.

Evidence of acquittal or conviction.

42.—(1) Where a person has been acquitted of an offence in the State, the fact of his or her acquittal, and any findings of fact made during the course of proceedings for the offence concerned, shall be admissible in evidence in a defamation action.

(2) Where a person has been convicted of an offence in the State, the fact of his or her conviction, and any findings of fact made during the course of proceedings for the offence concerned, shall be admissible in evidence in a defamation action.

Press Council

43.—(1) The Minister may by order declare that such body as is specified in the order shall be recognised for the purposes of this Act, and a body standing so recognised, for the time being, shall be known, and in this Act is referred to, as the "Press Council".

(2) Not more than one body shall stand recognised under this section for the time being.

(3) No body (other than a body that stands recognised under this section for the time being) shall be known as, or describe itself as, the Press Council.

(4) The Minister shall not make an order under *subsection (1)* unless he or she is satisfied that the body in respect of which he or she proposes to make the order complies with the minimum requirements specified in *Schedule* 2.

(5) If the Minister is of the opinion that a body for the time being standing recognised by order under this section no longer complies with the provisions of *Schedule* 2, he or she may revoke that order.

(6) The Minister shall, before making an order under *subsection (5)*, allow the body for the time being standing recognised under this section to make representations to him or her.

(7) Whenever an order is proposed to be made under this section a draft of the order shall be laid before each House of the Oireachtas and the order shall not be made unless a resolution approving of the draft has been passed by each such House.

SCHEDULE 1

Statements having Qualified Privilege

PART 1

Statements Privileged Without Explanation or Contradiction

1. A fair and accurate report of any matter to which the defence of absolute privilege would apply (other than a fair and accurate report referred to in *section 15(2)(i)* or *(j)*).

2. A fair and accurate report of any proceedings publicly heard before, or decision made public by a court (including a court-martial) established under the law of any state or place (other than the State or Northern Ireland).

3. A fair and accurate report of the proceedings (other than court proceedings) presided over by a judge of a court established under the law of Northern Ireland.

4. A fair and accurate report of any proceedings in public of a house of any legislature (including a subordinate or federal legislature) of any state other than the State.

5. A fair and accurate report of proceedings in public of any body duly appointed, in the State, on the authority of a Minister of the Government, the Government, the Oireachtas, either House of the Oireachtas or a court established under the Constitution to conduct a public inquiry on a matter of public importance.

6. A fair and accurate report of proceedings in public of any body duly appointed, in Northern Ireland, on the authority of a person or body corresponding to a person or body referred to in *paragraph 5* to conduct a public inquiry on a matter of public importance.

7. A fair and accurate report of any proceedings in public of any body—

(a) that is part of any legislature (including a subordinate or federal legislature) of any state (other than the State), or

(b) duly appointed in a state other than the State, on the authority of a person or body corresponding to a person or body referred to in *paragraph* 5,

to conduct a public inquiry on a matter of public importance.

8. A fair and accurate report of any proceedings in public of an international organisation of which the State or Government is a member or the proceedings of which are of interest to the State.

9. A fair and accurate report of any proceedings in public of any international conference to which the Government sends a representative or observer or at which governments of states (other than the State) are represented.

10. A fair and accurate copy or extract from any register kept in pursuance of any law which is open to inspection by the public or of any other document which is required by law to be open to inspection by the public.

11. A fair and accurate report, copy or summary of any notice or advertisement published by or on the authority of any court established by law in the State or under the law of a Member State of the European Union, or any judge or officer of such a court.

12. A fair and accurate report or copy or summary of any notice or other document issued for the information of the public by or on behalf of any Department of State for which a Minister of the Government is responsible, local authority or the Commissioner of the Garda Síochána, or by or on behalf of a corresponding department, authority or officer in a Member State of the European Union. 35

13. A fair and accurate report or copy or summary of any notice or document issued by or on the authority of a committee appointed by either House of the Oireachtas or jointly by both Houses of the Oireachtas.

14. A determination of the Press Ombudsman referred to in *paragraph 9(2)* of *Schedule* 2.

15. A determination of the Press Council referred to in *paragraph 9(4)* of *Schedule 2* or a report of the Press Council relating to the past performance of its functions.

16. Any statement published pursuant to, and in accordance with, a determination of the Press Ombudsman or the Press Council.

17. Any statement made during the investigation or hearing of a complaint by the Press Ombudsman in accordance with *Schedule* 2.

18. Any statement made during the hearing of an appeal from a determination of the Press Ombudsman in accordance with *Schedule* 2.

PART 2

Statements Privileged Subject to Explanation or Contradiction

1. A fair and accurate report of the proceedings, findings or decisions of an association, or a committee or governing body of an association, whether incorporated or not in the State or in a Member State of the European Union, relating to a member of the association or to a person subject, by contract or otherwise, to control by the association.

2. A fair and accurate report of the proceedings at any public meeting, held in the State or in a Member State of the European Union, being a meeting held for a lawful purpose and for the discussion of any matter of public concern whether the admission to the meeting is general or restricted.

3. A fair and accurate report of the proceedings at a general meeting, whether in the State or in a Member State of the European Union, of any company or association established by or under statute or incorporated by charter.

4. A fair and accurate report of the proceedings at any meeting or sitting of any local authority or the Health Service Executive, and any corresponding body in a Member State of the European Union.

5. A fair and accurate report of a press conference convened by or on behalf of a body to which this Part applies or the organisers of a public meeting within the meaning of *paragraph 2* to give an account to the public of the proceedings or meeting.

6. A fair and accurate report of a report to which the defence of qualified privilege would apply.

7. A copy or fair and accurate report or summary of any ruling, direction, report, investigation, statement (including any advice, admonition or censure given or administered by the Irish Takeover Panel under section 20 of the Irish Takeover Panel Act 1997) or notice made, given, prepared, published or served by the Irish Takeover Panel.

SCHEDULE 2

Minimum Requirements in Relation to Press Council

1. The Press Council shall be a company limited by guarantee.

2. The principal objects of the Press Council shall be to—

(*a*) ensure the protection of freedom of expression of the press,

(*b*) protect the public interest by ensuring ethical, accurate and truthful reporting by the press,

(*c*) maintain certain minimum ethical and professional standards among the press,

(*d*) ensure that the privacy and dignity of the individual is protected.

3. The Press Council shall be independent in the performance of its functions.

4. The owner of any periodical in circulation in the State or part of the State shall be entitled to be a member of the Press Council.

5. (1) The number of directors of the Press Council shall be 13, of whom—

(*a*) 7 shall be directors (in this Schedule referred to as

"independent public interest directors") who represent the public interest,

(b) 5 shall be directors who represent the interests of owners and publishers of periodicals,

(c) one shall be a director who represents the interests of journalists.

(2) One of the independent public interest directors of the Press Council shall be appointed as chairperson of the Press Council.

6. (1) The independent public interest directors shall—

(a) be persons who are of standing in the community,

(b) be persons who are independent of—

(i) the interests of owners and publishers of periodicals,
and

(ii) the interests of journalists,

and

(c) be selected for appointment as independent public interest directors—

(i) by a panel of persons who are, in the opinion of the Minister, independent of the interests referred to in *paragraph 5(1)(b)* and *(c)*,

(ii) in accordance with a selection process that is advertised to members of the public in a manner that the Minister considers to be sufficient.

(2) The criteria for selecting persons for appointment as independent public interest directors shall be published in such manner as will enable them to be inspected by members of the public.

7. (1) The Press Council shall be funded from subscriptions paid by members of the Press Council calculated in accordance with such rules as the Press Council shall make for that purpose.

(2) The Press Council shall not accept gifts or funding from any person other than subscriptions referred to in *subparagraph (1)*.

8. (1) The Press Council shall have authority to receive, hear and determine complaints concerning the conduct of its members.

(2) The Press Council shall appoint a person (in this Act referred to as the "Press Ombudsman") to investigate, hear and determine complaints made to the Press Council concerning the conduct of its members.

9. (1) The procedures for investigating, hearing and determining a complaint to the Press Ombudsman shall—

(a) where appropriate, provide for the expeditious and informal resolution of the matter between the complainant and the member of the Press Council in respect of whom the complaint was made,

(b) provide for the determination of the matter by the Press Ombudsman, where all reasonable efforts made in accordance with *clause (a)* in relation to the matter have failed,

(c) provide for the taking of remedial action by the member of the Press Council in respect of whom the complaint was made consisting of any or all of the following:

(i) the publication of the decision of the Press Ombudsman by such members of the Press Council as he or she directs and in such form and manner as he or she directs;

(ii) the publication of a correction of inaccurate facts or information relating to the complainant in a manner that gives due prominence to the correction in the publication concerned;

(iii) the publication of a retraction in respect of the material complained of; or

(iv) such other action as the Ombudsman may, in the circumstances, deem appropriate.

(2) A determination of the Press Ombudsman in relation to a complaint may be appealed to the Press Council.

(3) Where an appeal is brought against the determination of the Press Ombudsman it shall be determined by the directors of the Press Council.

(4) A determination of the Press Council, upon an appeal from a determination of the Press Ombudsman, shall be published by such members of the Press Council as the directors of the Press Council direct and in such form and manner as they direct.

10. The Press Council shall adopt a code of standards which shall specify the standards to be adhered to, and the rules and practices to be complied with by the members of the Press Council including—

(a) ethical standards and practices,

(b) rules and standards intended to ensure the accuracy of reporting where a person's reputation is likely to be affected, and

(c) rules and standards intended to ensure that intimidation and harassment of persons does not occur and that the privacy, integrity and dignity of the person is respected.

AN BILLE UM CHLÚMHILLEADH 2006

DEFAMATION BILL 2006

EXPLANATORY AND FINANCIAL MEMORANDUM

Purpose of the Bill

1. The purpose of the Bill is to revise in part the law of defamation and to replace the Defamation Act 1961 with modern updated provisions taking into account the jurisprudence of our courts and the European Court of Human Rights.

PART 1 — Preliminary and General

Short title and Commencement

2. *Section 1* is a standard provision and proposes that the Act shall come into operation on such day or days as the Minister may appoint by order.

Definitions

3. *Section 2* is a standard provision defining certain terms used in the Bill.

Saver

4. *Section 3* provides that the Act should only apply to a cause of action which accrues after it comes into operation. It also proposes that the Act shall not affect the operation of the general law in force immediately before the commencement of the Act.

Repeal

5. *Section 4* is self-explanatory.

PART 2 — Causes of Action

Defamation

6. *Section 5* collectively describes the tort of libel and the tort of slander as the tort of defamation and defines the essential ingredients of defamation. It also provides that the tort of defamation is actionable without proof of special damage.

Amendment of certain enactments

7. *Section 6* is self-explanatory.

Verifying affidavit

8. *Section 7* provides a mechanism whereby both the plaintiff and defendant are obliged to verify the particulars of any pleading containing assertions, allegations of fact or further information within a specific timeframe, which may be extended at the discretion of the court. The contents of the verifying affidavit could also form the subject matter for cross-examination of both plaintiff and defendant to which they must make themselves available at the time of the trial.

This section also provides for an offence if a person makes a statement in an affidavit that is false or misleading in any material respect or that he or she knows to be false or misleading.

Imputation

9. *Section 8* abolishes the existing rule of law under which each innuendo in a statement gives rise to a separate and distinct cause of action.

Defamation of class of persons

10. *Section 9* which seeks to clarify the existing law, provides that a member of a class of persons shall have a cause of action if by reason of the number of persons who are members of that class or by virtue of the circumstances in which the statement is published the statement could reasonably be understood to refer to the member concerned.

Multiple publication

11. *Section 10* provides for a general rule that only one cause of action will lie in respect of a multiple publication (as defined). It further provides that a court may allow a person to bring more than one defamation action in respect of multiple publication.

Defamation of a body corporate

12. *Section 11* provides that a body corporate may bring a defamation action whether or not it has incurred or is likely to incur financial loss as a result of the publication of the alleged defamatory statement.

Appeals in defamation actions

13. *Section 12* is self-explanatory.

Meaning

14. *Section 13* provides for a preliminary application to the court as to whether or not the matters complained of in defamation proceedings are reasonably capable of carrying the imputation pleaded by the plaintiff and, if so, whether that imputation is reasonably capable of bearing a defamatory meaning.

PART 3 — Defences

Truth

15. *Section 14* restates the existing law relating to the defence of justification which is now renamed the defence of truth.

Absolute Privilege

16. *Section 15* specifies a number of occasions where absolute privilege arises and is, for the most part, declaratory of the common law position in relation to these matters.

Qualified privilege

17. *Section 16* provides a statutory basis for the defence of qualified privilege.

Loss of defence of qualified privilege

18. *Section 17* deals with the circumstances in which a defendant loses the defence of qualified privilege and related matters.

Honest opinion

19. *Section 18* provides for a defence of honest opinion which is intended to replace the defence now known as fair comment.

Distinguishing between allegations of fact and opinion

20. *Section 19* sets out the criteria to be considered by a court when distinguishing between facts and opinion contained in a statement in defamation proceedings.

Offer to make amends

21. *Section 20* provides for a person who has published an allegedly defamatory statement to make an offer of amends. The offer shall not be made after a defence in the defamation action has been lodged. This section

updates the existing defence of unintentional defamation which is at present provided for in section 21 of the Defamation Act 1961.

Effect of offer to make amends

22. *Section 21* provides for the effect of acceptance or rejection of an offer to make amends. It updates the existing defence of unintentional defamation which is at present provided for in section 21 of the Defamation Act 1961.

Apology

23. *Section 22* provides that an offer of apology by a defendant to a plaintiff is not to be construed as an admission of liability.

Consent to publish

24. *Section 23* puts the common law defence of consent onto a statutory footing.

Fair and reasonable publication on a matter of public importance

25. *Section 24* introduces a new defamation defence into Irish law — the defence of fair and reasonable publication on a matter of public importance. It is essentially designed to facilitate public discussion where there is both a benefit and an interest in such discussion taking place. The defence is subject to the criterion of fairness and reasonableness and a range of matters — which are non-exhaustive — are specified which a court shall take into account in determining whether or not the publication of a statement is fair and reasonable in the circumstances. The defence is forfeited where the defendant believed the statement to be untrue, was actuated by bad faith, made out of spite or ill-will or other improper motive or that the statement bore no relation to the purpose of the defence and the manner and extent of the publication exceeded what was reasonably sufficient in all the circumstances.

Innocent publication

26. *Section 25* develops, in a more comprehensive way, the existing common law defence of innocent publication which has traditionally been available to distributors.

PART 4 — Remedies

Declaratory order

27. *Section 26* provides a new remedy for defamation to be known as a

declaratory order. It is intended to provide an expeditious avenue of redress where damages are not being sought.

Lodgement in Court

28. *Section 27* brings defamation proceedings into line with other actions for damages by allowing the defendant to lodge in court with the defence a sum of money in satisfaction of the plaintiff's claim. This lodgement may be made without admission of liability. *Subsection (3)* is intended to facilitate a plaintiff who may wish to ensure that some measure of public recognition attaches to the fact that the defendant was willing to settle the case before the trial of the action was concluded.

Correction Order

29. *Section 28* provides that where there is a finding that the statement in respect of which the action was taken was defamatory and the defendant has no defence to the action, the court may on the application of the plaintiff make an order directing the defendant to publish a correction of the defamatory statement. This correction order is a new remedy.

Damages

30. *Section 29* provides that parties in a defamation action may make submissions to the court in relation to damages. Where an action is brought in the High Court, the judge shall give directions to the jury in the matter of damages. *Subsection (4)* sets out a number of factors to which regard shall be had in making an award of general damages. The defendant may give certain evidence concerning the plaintiff for the purpose of mitigating damages.

Aggravated and punitive damages

31. *Section 30* broadly restates the current law by which the court has to award aggravated and punitive damages.

Dismissal for want of prosecution

32. *Section 31* provides that defamation proceedings in which no proceeding has been taken by the plaintiff for one year from the date they were commenced may be dismissed on application to the court by the defendant.

Order prohibiting the publication of a defamatory statement

33. *Section 32* sets out the grounds on which a court may grant or refuse

an order prohibiting the publication or further publication of defamatory matter.

Summary disposal of action

34. *Section 33* provides a mechanism whereby defamation proceedings may be disposed of in a summary fashion, on the application of the plaintiff, where the court is satisfied that the statement was defamatory and the defendant has no defence that is reasonably likely to succeed. The Court may also dismiss the action, upon the application of the defendant, where it is satisfied that the statement in respect of which the action was brought is not reasonably capable of being found to have a defamatory meaning.

PART 5 — Criminal Liability

Abolition of certain common law offences

35. *Section 34* is self-explanatory.

Publication of gravely harmful statements

36. *Section 35* creates a new offence of publication of gravely harmful statements. This applies where a person publishes a false statement causing grave injury to the reputation of the person and intended to cause that grave injury.

Seizure of copies of false statements

37. *Section 36* provides that where a person is convicted of an offence under *section* 35, a member of an Garda Siocha′ na may, on foot of a warrant issued by the court, enter and search a premises and seize copies of the statement in accordance with the terms of the warrant.

PART 6 — Miscellaneous

Limitation of defamation actions

38. *Section 37* provides that a one year limitation period shall apply in respect of defamation proceedings and related matters. Provision is also made in *subsection (1)* for the court to extend the period to 2 years in exceptional cases. Clarification is also provided as to when the cause of action accrues in respect of the matters which are dealt with in this section.

Survival of cause of action on death

39. *Section 38* provides that a cause of action in defamation should survive the death of the person in respect of whom the defamatory statement was

made. It also provides that a cause of action in defamation should survive the death of defamer.

Agreements for indemnity

40. *Section 39* is effectively a restatement of section 25 of the Defamation Act, 1961.

Jurisdiction of Courts

41. *Section 40* provides that, notwithstanding current jurisdiction limits, all defamation cases where the amount of the claim does not exceed €50,000 may be taken in the Circuit Court.

Malicious falsehood

42. *Section 41* is intended as a replacement for section 20 of the Defamation Act 1961. The provision clarifies both the basis of the tort and the circumstances where special damage is, or is not, required to be shown.

Evidence of acquittal or conviction

43. *Section 42* is evidential in nature and amends and clarifies the existing law relating to the admissibility of evidence of acquittals and convictions in defamation proceedings.

Press Council

44. *Section 43* provides that the Minister shall, on application to him, and having satisfied himself that the applicant materially complies with the minimum requirements prescribed in *Schedule* 2, make an order recognising the applicant as the Press Council. There can only be one such Press Council granted recognition at a time. This section also provides for the amendment or revocation of an order of recognition granted to the Press Council, should the Minister form the opinion that the Press Council no longer adheres to the minimum requirements prescribed in *Schedule 2*. The Press Council must be afforded the opportunity to address the matters of concern prior to the moving of any order. A draft of an order under *section 43* must be approved by both Houses of the Oireachtas before the order is made by the Minister.

Schedule 1 — Statements having qualified privilege

Schedule 1 provides for statements having qualified privilege. *Part 1* provides for statements privileged without explanation or contradiction. These include determinations or statements by the Press Council or

Ombudsman. *Part 2* provides for statements privileged subject to explanation or contradiction.

Schedule 2 — Minimum requirements in relation to Press Council

Schedule 2 provides for minimum requirements required of a body seeking recognition as the Press Council.

Financial Implications

45. There are no discernable financial implications for the Exchequer.

Index